MANSLATIONS

Decoding the Secret Language of Men

MANSLATIONS

JEFF MAC

SOURCEBOOKS, INC.®
NAPERVILLE, ILLINOIS

Published by Sourcebooks, Inc.
P.O. Box 4410, Naperville, Illinois 60567–4410
(630) 961–3900
Fax: (630) 961–2168
www.sourcebooks.com

Library of Congress Cataloging-in-Publication Data

Mac, Jeff.
   Manslations : decoding the secret language of men / Jeff Mac.
      p. cm.
   1. Man-woman relationships—Humor. 2. Men—Language. I. Title. II.
Title: Decoding the secret language of men. III. Title: Secret language of men.
   HQ801.M2338 2009
   306.708102'07—dc22
                                    2008018086

Printed and bound in the United States of America.
VP 10 9 8 7 6 5 4 3 2 1

This book is dedicated to all the ladies (and the occasional gentleman) who have written in to manslations.com—for the sheer optimism it must have taken to spill their guts to a total stranger over the Internet.

contents

WHAT IS A MANSLATION?

Boy, am I glad that you asked that. If you aren't interested in knowing at least that much, then I have to question why you've read even this far.

So a *man*slation is a *tran*slation (see what I did there?) of male behavior into something that a woman can understand. Here, I'll use it in a sentence:

"Wow, would you look at that *manslation* over there?"

And now I'll use it in a more helpful sentence: "Listen, when that guy told you—within thirty seconds of introducing himself at the bar—that he drives a hybrid because he cares about the environment, the *manslation* is that he was trying to work his way into your bikini areas."

Why Should You Care?

Because you are holding the Rosetta stone of relationships, conveniently printed on "paper." (I begged them to release my original stone draft, but there was something about shipping costs.)

Throughout this book, I will manslate some of the things men do and say—and then I'll teach you how to do it yourself. By the end, you will have the tools to manslate what any guy's doing or saying. Ultimately you won't even need me anymore, and I can go back to living my lifelong dream of sitting around at my place doing nothing.

But before we really get going, I'm sensing that you might have some questions for me, such as, who am I? Why should you listen to me? Why this book and not all the other books sitting on the shelf next to it? What do I weigh?

Well, have no fear. Not only am I going to answer these, but I am also going to make up the questions and pretend that I'm you. Convenient!

WHO ARE YOU AND WHY ARE YOU QUALIFIED TO WRITE THIS BOOK?

Firstly, I'm not sure I care for your tone. I wrote a *book,* is who I am. Then again, I guess that's a little bit like going on a job interview and, under references, putting your own phone number. Fair enough. It's a valid question.

I am the guy who can tell you how to understand all male behavior.

I know, I know. I don't expect you to just take my word for it. If you'll just bear with me, I'm going to dump virtual bucket loads of authority all over the place.

Why should you consider me "qualified"? Because of the almost legendary abilities of stand-up comics to maintain healthy relationships?* Because you've always wanted to get dating advice from someone who was once paid to be the voice of a package of toilet paper? How about because I write an online daily advice column answering any and all questions that women have about men? Okay, getting warmer…

---

* You might have seen me on Comedy Central's show *Live at Gotham.* This is especially likely if you were looking at your TV during my set.

Here are some of the real reasons why you should listen to me (besides common courtesy).

All Human Males Know How to Read Other Human Males

And, I suspect, all other male animals, as we'll discuss later. All men instinctively know what's going on with other men. Yes, it's absolutely true. Every time you've found yourself confused, bewildered, baffled, stymied, perhaps even bamboozled or hoodwinked by a man, virtually every other man around knew precisely what was happening. And they didn't tell you.

On behalf of all the nice guys out there, we're sorry about that. We're sorry that we never told you why this guy insisted he would call you and then didn't, or why that guy got furious with you that time when you caught him cheating. We could have told you, but we didn't. We're sorry. We're really, really sorry.

In our own defense, our reasons for not telling you were… okay, they were really cowardly. It's not much of a defense, I know.

What are you saying? Why wouldn't even my nice guy friends explain this stuff for me?

The reason that you can't get a decent manslation from the vast majority of the men in your life—even the really super nice ones—is this: the men who know you are all in one or both of the following two categories:

1. The guys who know that tattletaling on another guy doesn't look very manly

2. The guys who want to sleep with you

Lucky for you, I fall into neither of those categories. Not only have I long ago given up on being considered manly, but I don't want to sleep with you. A man can't offer you a true manslation unless he is completely willing to NOT sleep with you. Otherwise, he won't be able to be honest for fear that it might jeopardize his chances of gaining access to your boobs.

How come you're not trying to sleep with us?

Look, I'm sure you'd be great at it and all. It's just that, well, first of all I'm in a relationship with pretty much the perfect woman. And even if I were stupid enough to risk that by sleeping with you, she would—how do you say?—"murder us both and make it look like an accident."

Okay, so you don't want to sleep with us. What else you got?

I'm glad you asked.

I've been in several long-term relationships (although some of them probably just seemed really long). Most of them didn't work out, of course. Well, obviously none of them did except for the current one, which, let's face it, we still don't know for sure, right?

But that's not the point.

The point is that I have information. I've seen the other side. I've been let into the inner sanctum. Once you are with a woman for long enough, the veil comes down. She realizes that you are no longer on the "other team." The differences between your genitals become less important. You are awarded an honorary vagina. And you wear it on your sleeve.

That's my point. I wear a vagina on my sleeve.

During one particularly long relationship, I basically ceased to be a man altogether. Unless the toilet needed to be fixed or something, I was just one of the girls. No, that's not even right. I was like a pet man on the Planet of the Women. This might sound fun (it is!), or like some soft-core porn they show on *Cinemax After Dark* (it's not!).

During this time, some of my female friends started to ask me to interpret male behavior. They would trust me with their side of things, because, hey, who was I going to tell? I no longer had any male friends. (I know why the caged man sings).

The more and more shocking conversations that I had with female friends, the more I knew that I had to help. Even some of my smartest friends would show such a stunning inability to understand men that I just had to do something.

So I became a manslator. Of course it was wrong. I was betraying my brothers. I only hope that the men of the world can forgive me, if anyone ever tells them that this book exists. Either that or I hope that when they are on their way to my place to beat me up, they get lost and refuse to ask for directions.

But in all fairness, the "secret language of men" needs about as much translating as a coloring book once you know what you're looking at. But my lady friends didn't.

And I do.

And now you will, too.

My Main Qualifications

Ah yes, my professional qualifications as a manslator? None, really. I have no formal training. Or formal clothing, for that matter. I have no background in math or science. (The last "science" class I took was Nutrition for Actors, and the professor was morbidly obese. Seriously.)

I have what every man has: an uncomfortable awareness of how easy men are to read and interpret.

But I've also got something that most men don't have: zillions of women who have already asked all of your questions about men. At www.manslations.com, I get letters every day from women who need answers. I've heard it all. I know what confuses you people about us. And over time, I've learned how to explain our (painfully simple) male ways in words that make sense to women. And I'm willing to tell you all about it.

I am like those scientists at Los Alamos working on the Manhattan Project in that (a) I'm not at all concerned about the dangerous forces I'm fooling with, and (b) if you dropped this book from an airplane, it would almost certainly hurt any person it landed on. In my later years, I expect that I, like Oppenheimer, will deeply regret the role that I played in the opening of such a Pandora's box without a moment's thought for all the poor, unsuspecting people who will never know what hit them.*

---

* I have been blessed/cursed in that people I meet need to tell me about their deepest, most embarrassing problems. I'm not sure if I give off a smell or what. I think it's probably just that they sense that I'm a good listener. And luckily, they don't know that the reason I'm such a great listener is only that I'm trying to get all the details down so I can get their story right later on when I'm telling the first person I think will laugh the loudest.

YOU NEVER FORGET YOUR FIRST TIME

Here are a couple examples of some of the very first manslations I ever… uh… administered?… to give you an idea of what I'm talking about.

I had a friend who I consider to be a very smart, contemplative person. One night while waiting tables in New York City, one of her male customers struck up a conversation with her that continued throughout his meal. At one point, he mentioned that he was flying to Bermuda with a few friends in his private plane and did she want to go? You know, no biggie.

Now… I'm having a hard time even typing this part. She didn't think that this man was necessarily trying to have sex with her.

Had that story been about an eleven-year-old girl who had grown up in a cave, raised by wolves or badgers or something, you'd hear that last part and think, "Oh, that poor thing. Shame on that bad, bad man for trying to take advantage of her lack of experience like that."

But this was an intelligent woman, an artist—a New Yorker, no less.

I asked this young woman, "So, ah, what do you think he wanted when he asked you that?" I really tried not to sound like I was asking the equivalent of, "Now, when you slammed your hand in that door, er, how did you think that might feel? Good or… less good?"

"Maybe he was just being nice!" she said. "Some people do that, you know. Every man doesn't want to sleep with every woman he meets!" And she rolled her eyes.

You know—as if I was the one being naïve.

So when this "just being nice" man showed up at her restaurant again the following week and asked her if she wanted to go back to his hotel room, she was shocked—shocked, I say!—that his trip to Bermuda had been a cover to get him laid. Of course, any man could have spotted this guy's agenda from across the street. (Hint: when a guy says something wildly impressive and passes it off like it's no big deal… well, just hang onto your pants is all I'm saying.)

Another example: A good friend came to me crying, bewildered, because her boyfriend had left town saying he loved her, and then came back a week later saying, "I just don't know if I can be a good boyfriend right now."

Now…that guy cheated on her. That's not a guess. It's a fact. But she made the classic mistake of listening to what he *said* rather than paying attention to what he *did*. And I knew that I could help her understand what was going on. So I did.

And, of course, a month later, after they had broken up, she learned that he *had* cheated on her during that week away. Again—bewildering to her, but obvious to any man. In this book, you'll learn to see this kind of stuff as we guys do.

So why should I buy this book instead of the fifty others on the shelf right beside it? What's so special about this one?

Look, there are already plenty of books like

1. Guides to help you tell when a guy you don't know very well doesn't like you very much. (Vital to be able to do, of course. However, it's pretty simple once you read the next chapter of this book.)

2. Guides to help you spot total womanizing jerks. (Again, very important to be able to do. But not only is this also pretty easy to do, it only helps you locate jerks. If you meet a guy who is not a jerk, it doesn't really help you deal with him.)

3. Self-help books written by psychologists who can tell you all about how a man's mommy issues are ultimately going to wind up becoming your issues. (The only problem with that seems to be that no matter how informative the books are…well…the guy still has mommy issues, right?)

4. Books to help you trick a man into marrying you by following rules, such as pretending you don't like him very much. (Yeah, that one still confuses me. Oh, unless you're seven years old. Then it might work.)

This book isn't any of these. I'm not a womanizer (much to my eternal embarrassment, I've always been lousy at meaningless sex). And besides, knowing how to spot an a-hole isn't the beginning and the end of dating, is it?

Here are a couple of quick examples of the kind of bone-headed advice I'm trying to counteract single-handedly:

MANSLATIONS CHART: WHAT THEY SAY VS.

Question:	Your Average Trashy Women's Magazine	Self-Help Books Written by Other Men	Your Mom
We had a great date; should I call him?	Send him an embarrassingly sexy text message explaining what you want to do to him on your NEXT date!	If he wanted to hear from you, he'd call YOU. And you rock, and you shouldn't have to call dudes.	A woman should NEVER call a man—it looks so needy. And eat something; you're looking pale.
I saw him totally checking out another woman's boobs!	Wear something trashy as hell and keep his attention on YOUR boobs!	Your boobs rock, and a man who rocks will be into them enough to notice that.	If a man is getting what he needs at home, he doesn't look elsewhere. Oh, and clean your room.
He won't talk to me about his feelings.	Umm…talk?	You really rock.	That's what you have ME for!
I really want him to buy me flowers sometimes. Why doesn't he ever think of that?	When he comes home, be on the bed wearing fresh flower petals and nothing else! He'll get the message!	Why flowers? What did he do wrong? (Furthermore, you rock out, and you deserve flowers.)	Buy yourself flowers, sweetie. And get some for me while you're there.
So…how DO you drive a man wild in bed?	Put a mint in your mouth when you go down on him!	By rocking out.	(passes out)

MANSLATIONS ANSWERS

Your Girlfriends	Manslations Answer!
Don't call him too soon—you don't want to scare him off.	If you want to call him, call him. If he likes you, it will help, and if he doesn't...uh...who cares? If it's been more than 2 days, though, don't bother. He didn't think your date was "great." No, there are no exceptions.
What a jerk! You should totally call him on it. Make him squirm.	Pretend you didn't notice. He can't help it, but it doesn't mean anything. We all do it. If you want to avoid SEEING it, feel free to tell him (NOT then, but during a coolheaded moment), "Hey listen, I know you look at boobs, just never let me notice it, ok? It would bug me." But try to get used to the idea that all men will always do this forever. Not just the jerks.
He's probably just afraid of vulnerability.	Why SHOULD he talk about his feelings? If there's some reason for him to talk about them, he'll talk about them. What do you REALLY want from him? Attention? Affection? Closeness? Ask for that, instead.
Buy HIM flowers and cards and stuff. Then maybe he'll get the message.	Never buy him something he doesn't want so he'll figure out that you want him to buy YOU that thing. What is that, a hint? He'll never get it. You have to explain it to him, and you'll get your flowers. I know you want him to just KNOW, but he doesn't. And he never will.
Wear sexy lingerie and ...um...I read about this weird mint thing in *Cosmo*...	Look, if you are currently alive and IN his bed, he's already halfway wild right there. After that, if YOU'RE having a fantastic time, and you pay attention to him, he'll be plenty wild, I promise. And if you really want to do the weird mint trick, hey, knock yourself out.

I'm not a psychologist, though I have to admit that it does seem mildly attractive to charge somebody 150 bucks an hour to sit there and let *them* talk to *you*. I'm not trying to give you "ammunition" that you can use against men—we're already obscenely outmatched by women as it is. I'm just a nice, normal man you might meet on, you know, the Earth. And I wanted to offer women something a little different from all of that.

Since it's so simple for men to read and understand the behavior of other men, I wanted to share with women my experience in how to do it. It's not just about how to get a date or how to get a husband. *It's about how to understand men—any man—and understand who it is you're dealing with, even when he won't (or can't) tell you himself.*

Plus, as if that isn't enough reason to sell you on *Manslations*, check *this* out—you're already *reading* it. Purely from the standpoint of convenience, I'd say that's tough to beat.

HOW TO USE THIS BOOK

I've seen this sort of section listed in the introductions of other books. Honestly, I'm not sure how many ways there *are* to use a book. Well, other than to say that you should probably read the words. I think you'll find it makes a very real difference in your appreciation of the book.

If you can think of any other ways to use the book, though, feel free to write them in the margins here. (Please make sure you've paid for it first. Bookstores tend to frown on that sort of thing if you don't already, you know, "own" the book. Boy, did I find *that* out the hard way.)

basic manslations theory,
or the stuff you don't know

Okay, in the interest of full disclosure, this is kind of
a trick title. All manslations theory is basic. I know
that some women love to believe that there are complex and
fantastical explanations and excuses for various male behavior
patterns. (And if you want to hear a few, just ask any woman
who is having an affair with a married man. She's got *piles* of
that stuff.) But in most cases, men are very, very easy to read
if you know how to do it.

Lucky for you, it won't take long to learn absolutely
everything you need to know to understand all the men in
your life. (And the ones in other people's lives, if you've got
some spare time on your hands or if you're waiting at the
airport or something.)

Behold: The Five Supreme Laws of Manslation*

I know it seems like an oversimplification to say that all
male behavior can be explained with only five things—but in
truth, even five is probably giving us too much credit. Most
stuff can be explained using just one or two of these at a time.
But you get all five, so now you'll be prepared for everything
and anything.

---

* Technically, it's Three Principles, a Golden Rule, and Two Big Questions. But
you can't introduce that with "Behold."

Well, except for the thing where some guys like to fart on each other. You're on your own there.

THE POINTY-STICK-PROBLEM-SOLVER PRINCIPLE

Where does male thinking come from? (And can we send it back?)

Ha ha ha ha. Oh ho ho ho! Oh! Oh, you!

No, but seriously. Where does male thinking come from?

To explain, we have to go back to caveman times.*

When there were problems in the caveman world, they were mostly physical problems. Things like, "Mother *eff*, is it ever cold in this cave!" or, "Holy cow, would you just look at the size of that bear that's coming into our cave. What are we going to do about this huge ani—?"

So the biggest, strongest cave folks (i.e., the men) would have to run out there with clubs or sticks and do something about it. And if they couldn't, people would die, and nobody would snuggle up next to them during the long caveman nights.

Or when someone said something like, "Hey, I think I'm getting hungry for dinner," there would be grumblings about how delicious that elk had looked yesterday,

---

* Not literally, you understand. I'm just saying that we're going to talk about it. Believe me, if I could actually transport us back through time, I'd be so rich I wouldn't even have to be an author. Plus I'd be too busy running around, stopping Hitler, righting wrongs, betting on sporting events of which I already knew the winners, and making sure my parents met at the "Enchantment Under the Sea" dance in time to get the DeLorean to the old clock tower.

all antlery and jumpy aroundy, and so unlike that bowl of
twigs we had for breakfast.

Once again, who had the honor of chasing down that
elk and stabbing it with a pointy stick? You guessed it. The
bigger, more muscled folks—the men. As a result of all of this
running around, hitting, poking, hunting, etc., the male mind
evolved into a problem solver. His value was based around
whether or not he could *do* stuff *about* stuff *with* stuff.

Now, fast-forward to today. Men are still trying to solve
problems. But the problems are different. We almost never
battle with wild animals anymore. (Probably for the best, if
you think about it. I've seen TV shows where some creature
gets loose at a zoo or something and battles with a human.
It almost always goes badly for whichever one happens to be
wearing the polo shirt.)

So with no giant beasts to fight, when a woman says
something like, "I feel fat," the man will snap into action and
attempt to poke the problem to death with the pointy stick
of his little mind, telling her how she is *not* fat—what is she,
crazy?—she's perfect just the way she is—what is she talking
about "fat"? Even when, wow, she sure is.

In the cave-ish portion of his brain, the man has defined a
problem ("Something's wrong—we aren't watching football"),
and he's working feverishly on a solution ("Please, what can
I say so we can stop talking about this in time for the fourth
quarter").

This ancient style of problem solving doesn't always help
a man become very *good* at thinking of a solution today, especially since your garden-variety modern problem isn't going
to require a spear. (Though God knows I've had moments

on the subway when I'm positive that a spear would help.) Sometimes his "problem-solver side" goes after the wrong thing entirely and needs some help.

You might see this when you're discussing a problem with your man. You're talking about work; you're frustrated; you're feeling underappreciated; you're upset with your boss; and you're not sure if you even want this job anyway. What's your man doing? Listing off eleven different ways you could make this situation better. And you want to kill him because HE'S NOT LISTENING...

Well, he *is* listening. Just not in the way you need. He has identified what he feels is the appropriate elk (your job problems) ripe for the stick-poking (getting you a different job, telling your boss you want a transfer, whatever).

Solution? Give him a different elk. Tell him, "I have a problem, and I need your help. What I need most is for you to just listen to me, let me vent, and don't try to solve the problem yet. That will really help me." He'll poke and club that problem to death like you won't believe.

THE JACK BAUER PRINCIPLE

So, men have left behind the caves, the pointy sticks, the fur bathing suits of their ancestors in the days of yore (most men, anyway). But in addition to the mad pointy-stick-problem-solving skills, men can trace another trait back to the cave, and it is this: Men still have some kind of a weird biological memory of being badasses. Think about it. One of our ancestors must have been a badass, or else everybody in that cave would have bit the dust. (Yes, I realize that everybody in that cave *did* bite the dust, but you can't blame men for that. Simple biology, people.)

So what does the fact that our progenitors were ancient badasses have to do with, say, a modern accountant? Or a computer programmer? Much like the spearing of your odd elk, there's not much call for badass-ery in most of modern life. Your ability to fight a woolly mammoth with your bare hands is less in demand than, say, knowing how to order properly at Starbucks.

According to the most brilliant minds in this field,* the badass tendency didn't go anywhere. It's still there, lying dormant in most men. Thus...

Every man secretly believes that he's just a few sit-ups away from being *24*'s Jack Bauer.

We're all pretty sure that one day the Navy SEALs are going to call up and say, "We're under attack—we just lost half our squad! We need *you!*" And by God, we'll be ready.**

Now... consciously, intellectually, we know that not only are the Navy SEALs never going to call, but we would *not* be ready if they did. However, we still wish we were badasses.

It's very, very important for women to understand this about men. If you follow this, then you know why he doesn't want to, say, go clothes shopping with you.

---

* Regarding the "brilliant minds in this field" of manslations theory, I can say two things definitively. One, I am the only mind in the field, and so I can claim to be the most brilliant one. And two, for any kids who want to grow up and work in the manslations field, I'd say you're better off renting office space. It gets cold, manslating in a field.
** The Jack Bauer Principle is why men are so jealous of firemen. First of all, they're actually doing all the stuff that we wish we were doing. And second, we know that women look at firemen in the same way that men look at...well...all women.

Imagine your Jack Bauers of the world (or your average Navy SEAL, Green Beret, ninja, or Jedi) picking out blouses with his girlfriend. You can't, can you? That's just not much of a "mission." These men have no time for blouses—they're all rappelling down the side of a building or kicking in a door or punching an evil person in the stomach or something.

I'm not saying that your man actually wishes he was *doing* these things, but he likes the idea that he might be considered capable of them. He doesn't want anything to interfere with that fantasy. Like shopping with you, for example.

Let's take that a little further.

What do you do if you want him to come shopping with you? Well first of all, don't want that. If he's anything like me, he will be an infuriating shopper. He's not your girl-friend. He's your man. He won't be very helpful.

However if you *must* take him shopping, you can't nag him into it. It will never work. You have to make him feel like *more* of a badass for coming along than if he had just refused and stayed home. If you can somehow convince him that the very fact that he's doing this stuff makes him *more* of a man than those "sissies who refuse to go shopping with their girlfriends to prove what *men* they are," you'll have much better results.

Juvenile? Yes. Silly? Probably. Embarrassing? Sure. But it will work better than nagging, "Why can't you ever just come shopping!?" He's heard this before. From his mom. And the moment he heard it was when he first began to suspect that he was never going to be rappelling down anything.

This is just one example of the Jack Bauer Principle. We'll see it again a little later. Just trust me—if you can understand this about your man, you'll be so much happier. So will he. In these moments, let it be a little less like, "Will you stop being such an idiot and just do what I want?" and a little more like, "Help me, Obi-Wan Kenobi. You're my only hope." I think you'll be pleased with the results.

THE WHAT IT DOES VS. WHAT IT MEANS PRINCIPLE

Speaking in broad stereotypes, men seem to interpret the world and the stuff in it in terms of what it *does*, or its utility. This is why guys go crazy about tools. They have a function. They *do*. The broad, stereotypical female reaction to a thing is to ask what it *means*, or its significance.

Take, for example, the humble thank-you card. The thank-you card is primarily designed for its meaning, and as a result, men are not the best gender at remembering to send them (though in our defense, we're in the top two). Nor do we really care about receiving them. We just don't get it.

The reason is that they don't do anything. Whenever I get one of these cards from someone, I never know what I'm supposed to do with it. I'm always thinking, "What are we up to here? What is this card supposed to get me to do? She already said thank you in person. So what's this about? What was wrong with *that* thank you? Should I acknowledge this card? Am I supposed to send a card back to her, thanking her for this card that thanked me? When does it stop? Am I in trouble?" And then I need to go to bed.

Now, most women just assume that this is a nice, *meaningful* thing to do, to show someone that you are grateful, that you care, that whatever you're thanking them for *meant* something to you.

For me, and for a lot of men, thank-you cards are like vitamins. I'm not sure what they do; I don't really understand them; but I'm pretty sure I have to use them or else something vaguely bad might happen. (The difference, of course, is that failure to use one of these things might result in someone's feelings being hurt, and in the other case, my gums might fall out or something.)

The next two sections are the biggest, most important things ever. Ever? Yes, ever. If you can really take this stuff in, you're going to cut down on the "*what the hell is he thinking*" part of your life drastically. You'll have so much free time on your hands, you'll be able to knit a twenty-foot image of me and use it as a slipcover for your garage. (Or you could do something not creepy. Your choice!)

THE MANSLATOR'S GOLDEN RULE

On my website, I get all kinds of questions from women complaining that a man is sending them "mixed signals."

Here are a few examples:

- He says, "I had a great time—I'll call you," but then doesn't.

- He says, "No, nothing's wrong," but he won't spend any time with you.

- He says he wants a "real relationship," but you only hear from him at 3:00 a.m., when he's drunk and wants to come over for sex.

- He says noncommittal things or not much at all, but he keeps finding reasons to spend time with you.

- He says he's psyched to hang out with your friends but constantly "forgets" what night you're getting together with them and makes other plans.

None of these situations are mysterious to a man. Any man can tell you without hesitation that these signals aren't mixed, blended, or even lightly stirred. In fact, most men wouldn't even know what could possibly have confused you.

Here's the Manslator's Golden Rule, which will solve all of these "puzzles."

Ready?

Whenever there is any conflict between what a man says and what he does, always, always ignore what he says.

Okay, now read it again. Yes, I do mean "always." If you can really understand this much about your man, you'll probably know even more about him than *he* does.

See, we males don't always know what's going on with us any better than you do. Hell, when we're talking about how we think or feel, we're barely listening ourselves. A decent percentage of what we say in those situations is going to be a load of crap that we're throwing out there in hopes that by saying it, it will be true. But our behavior? That doesn't lie.

Imagine your dog. Good, now imagine somebody else's dog. Excellent! What a good imagination you have.

No, but seriously, think of a dog when it's happy. Now, is it hard to "read" what's going on with that dog? Not really. That dog might not even know he's happy, but you sure know it. Same with men, except we can talk. Plus we don't pee on the ground. (Most of the time, anyway. Okay, sometimes in an emergency or as a signature in a snowbank.)

I've been in plenty of situations where I've said (and believed) that "nothing's wrong" and I "didn't want to break up," but my legs (who don't take orders from the same guy that controls my mouth) were already walking, telling me, "Sorry, pally. It's time to am-scray, vamoose, twenty-three skiddoo."*

If you can remember to pay attention to what a man is *doing*, you will never again need to be confused by what he's saying. Behavior tells the truth. There is zero point in using a man's words to figure out where he's at. You might as well ask your dog those questions they have at the end of *Inside the Actors Studio*. **

THE TWO BIG QUESTIONS

So now that we've established that a man's behavior tells the truth, let's talk a little bit about how to interpret that behavior.

If you find yourself wondering how a man feels about you... stop wondering. Just leave your wonderer on pause, because it's obvious how he feels about you. Look at his behavior (and, as we said, *not* his words) and ask yourself two questions:

1. Might he think*** that this behavior will get him laid?

---

* It was on these occasions that I realized my legs are mobsters from 1928. That's a tough day in any man's life. But I handled it with aplomb, people.

** I wouldn't recommend asking your dog those questions. I'm not an expert on dogs, but I'm pretty sure that your dog's not famous, so who cares what his favorite curse word is?

*** Please remember that I've added in the concept of what he "might think" in both of the Two Big Questions. We're looking for his motivation here, but we are not necessarily saying that he knows what the hell he's talking about. It's entirely possible that there is some man somewhere who thinks that by pouring motor oil in your hair, he's going to convince you to sleep with him. (And if that's your boyfriend, congratulations!)

2. Might he think that this behavior will maximize his time with you?

That's it. These are the two keys to interpreting all male behavior. And yes, you need both, or it's no good. If you've seen as many movies that involve the firing of nuclear missiles as I have (i.e., "all of them"), then you know that they require *two* keys to launch. If only one of the guys uses his key, you can't launch anything. At that point, all you can do is yell at the other guy to put in that second key (which, if he does, will then require Jack Bauer to get there quickly and start punching).*

Let's break it down.

- If the answer to the Two Big Questions is "no," then he doesn't like you.

- If the answer to number one is yes and number two is no, he wants to have sex with you but doesn't like you that much.

- If the answer to number two is yes and number one is no, he's a close relative. Or a woman. Or an itinerant eunuch. Whatever he is, he's probably not your man.

Why these two questions? On its own, the first question is not an indicator of anything other than exactly what it says. Knowing that a man wants to have sex with you doesn't tell you much. It tells you that he thinks that having sex with you might be fun (and who am I to argue with him?).

---

* I realize that the metaphor at this point involves the launch of nuclear weapons. I'm sure most relationship situations aren't quite to that level. Most.

A lot of women stop here. "He wants me like crazy. He must really like me." This is a huge misconception, and we'll get deeper into it in the next chapter. But for now, just know that sexual attraction for a man has zero to do with liking you. Any man is perfectly capable of desiring a sexual encounter with a woman whom he actively dislikes. Yes. Any man. That doesn't mean that all men pursue sex with women they don't like. All I'm saying is there's no link between wanting to have sex with a woman and liking anything else about her.

Now, from my experience with telling women about this, I can hear some of you out there right now:

He's generalizing. I don't believe that all men are really like that.

I know you don't believe it. That's how men get you into bed, even when you're way out of their league. That's why you need this book—to keep your bed (and your life) stocked with only the finest, most worthy men.

So if his sexual desire for you doesn't tell you anything, how do we know if he likes you? That's where the second question comes in.

What does maximizing his time spent with you have to do with anything? Answer: A "player" wants to do the opposite. A guy who only wants to have sex with you will spend as little non-sex time with you as he can get away with. He'll put in *exactly* what he believes is the bare minimum of effort required to remove any and all obstacles to humping (i.e., suspicion, sobriety, good judgment, morals, standards, underwear, what have you).

On the other hand, if a guy likes you, if he wants to date you or wants to have a relationship, you'll see him wanting to spend *more* time with you, not less. This (and not just his sexual interest) is how you tell how much a man likes you (the answers vary from "not at all" to "restraining order").

Anyway, that's it. That's truly, seriously, honestly all you need to know to figure out whether or not he likes you.

REAL MANSLATIONS EXAMPLES FROM THE DATING TRENCHES*

Now, once again, I can hear you out there:

No, you don't understand. My situation is more complex.

No. If you are wracking your brains about why a man is behaving as he is, trust me, you are almost certainly wracking the wrong thing.

Let's take a look at one of the most obvious examples from real life where we can apply what we're talking about—the "booty call."

So let's say that you met a guy at a bar. You flirt, you talk, you laugh. He asks for your number. He tells you that he's going to call you. You go home thinking that you're going to hear from him. But you do not. Not the next day and not the day after that. But then, three weeks later, he calls you at eleven thirty at night and says that he has been thinking of

---

* Totally metaphorical trenches here. I don't recommend dating in actual trenches. Then again, if you've got a World War I fetish or something, hey, who am I to stop you?

you since the two of you met. He said he had wanted to call you, but he couldn't get up the nerve. But he really liked you, he just hasn't been able to get you off his mind, he wants to see you—and what are you doing right now?

Now, this conversation is never not a booty call. Why?

First, the Golden Rule

Is there a conflict between what he said and what he did? Yes, there sure is. He *said* he would call you but *did,* you know, other things that were not calling. He then *said* he couldn't stop thinking about you, blah blah blah. But that still doesn't change the fact that what he *did* was not call you. For three weeks. Until eleven thirty at night.

So given that a discrepancy exists between what he said and what he did, we can follow the golden rule and focus solely on his behavior—the DID part. Here's what he did:

- Got your number

- Did not call for three weeks (even though he could have at any moment)

- Finally called you at 11:30 p.m.

- Attempted to get together with you right then

The Two Big Questions

Let's analyze that stuff using our two questions.

1. Might he think that this behavior will get him laid? Yep. That's certainly the most desirable ending to the evening from his perspective.

2. Might he think that this behavior will maximize his time with you? Nope. He had your number. If spending a lot of time with you was a priority, why did he deprive himself of you for three weeks? And why did he wait until the middle of the night? The answer is that he wants to spend as little non-sex time with you as humanly possible.

This guy wanted to do you, and if you did it, you likely won't hear from him again. Well, maybe in another few weeks if he thought he could get away with it again.

I'm not trying to depress you. I just want you to be able to spot a douche when you see one. And that's how you do it.

But what if the guy isn't a douche? (Hey, it happens.) Same rules apply. Let's look at another example—this time, one based on a question I got at manslations.com.

A woman wrote to me concerned that her man wouldn't tell her how he felt about her. When they met, they lived in separate countries, but soon they were calling, emailing, and even making regular international visits. He asked her to be his girlfriend, and they became exclusive. He asked her to move to his country when she finished grad school.

All this, but he would not talk about his feelings for her, even when she asked. He said that he was a "very private person" and didn't like "being probed for information."*

She didn't want to consider moving to be closer to him unless he was in love with her, so she wrote to me for help.

How do we manslate this situation? First, the Golden Rule. Are his words and actions contradictory? Yes, they sure

---

* Most men don't like to be probed at all. Just ask any alien abductees you know.

seem to be. So let's forget all about what he does or doesn't *say* for a moment and focus on what he's doing:

- Contacting her all the time (calling, emailing, etc.)
- Visiting her from another country
- Asking her to date exclusively and not pursuing any other women
- Trying to get her to move in with him when she graduates

Now, the Two Big Questions:

1. Might he think this is going to get him laid? Yep. (And as a side note, I bet he's absolutely correct.)

2. Might he think this is going to get him some more time with her? Yes, it is. He's doing everything he can to spend as much time with her (and only her) as humanly possible and to make sure that she's not seeing other men.

Verdict: Even though this guy doesn't like to talk about his feelings, we all know exactly what they are. He's with her for real. There's no other great explanation for all the behavior.

I understand that she might really want or need him to talk about his feelings for her at some point. And of course there's nothing wrong with that. Totally reasonable desire. She's just going to have to teach him why that's important. (See Chapter 7, "Having 'The Talk.'")

REALLY. IT'S THAT SIMPLE.

I know that you don't believe it's this simple, but I promise that's all you need to know. If you can really grasp the Five Supreme Laws of Manslation, you'll go a long way toward understanding all the men in your life. And if you choose to ignore those things, hey, no skin off my nose, you know? It works with global warming, right? Oh... wait...

CHAPTER 2 • of myths and men, or stuff
you don't even know
you don't know

et's look at some of the main myths that women believe
about men, shall we? I really think we should, or else the
chapter title won't make any sense at all.*
Ready? Let's go!

THERE MUST BE SOME MYTHUNDERSTAND-ING

MYTH: Men Are Afraid of Commitment.

FACT: I have no idea what this one even means. It's non-sense. Total nonsense. I'll admit that men are afraid of com-mitting to someone they don't want to be with. But, um, isn't everyone? Seems like sort of a healthy fear, like the ones we have of "fire" or of "getting stuck in a conversation with your friend's boring grandfather."

---

*When I say "myths," I'm not talking about the kind that involve Zeus, Thor, or a flying snake with wings that asks Aztecs to do human sacrifices. That stuff is just weird and probably not very useful here. What I'm talking about are the stories told from generation to generation to annoy people who don't know them. They involve stuff that isn't true, such as when people say something like, "No, dude, Bigfoot is real," or, "I read this Eastern philosophy book that said men can have multiple orgasms." That's one of the best things about a myth: once you know it's only a myth, you can say, "Pff, that's just a myth," and be totally right. And make them feel like real jerks.

Men want to be with someone they want to be with. And if we are with the right person, well, of course we're going to want to *stay* with her. But if we aren't sure we want to be there (which usually ends up meaning that we don't), yeah, that's when you'll get some "fear of commitment." This is sometimes also known as "not liking you."

I can remember a relationship I was in many, many years ago. I could feel the "commitment heat" coming off of her. She wanted to talk about moving in together. I was a little panicky about the whole thing. And for a minute there, I thought that there was something wrong with *me* because I was afraid to commit to her. I actually had the following thought:

"Oh, man. I guess I'm with the woman I'm going to be with forever, and I don't really like her. This blows."

And so it did.

It was only later when I was in a good relationship that I realized, "Hmm. Weird. I have no problem committing in this situation—one that I want to be in. Odd, huh? Probably just a coincidence."

I promise there are no men who think, "This situation is perfect. I'm with the perfect woman for me. I love spending time with her. But I am afraid of commitment, and so I will leave her." Honestly, that doesn't happen in the real world, where we live and work and pay bills. If a man wants out, it's because he wants out. It's not because you're too perfect for him.

Remember the Manslator's Golden Rule: if he's backing out the door but saying how perfect you are... er... which one of those things do you think you should believe?

MYTH: If a Man Isn't Psyched about Planning Our Wedding, He Isn't Truly Committed.

FACT: If a man isn't psyched about *being married*, he isn't truly committed. But planning the wedding ceremony itself? Most men aren't going to be all that psyched about that whole day. Why not? Well, weddings aren't very manly, are they? No. Can you picture Jack Bauer at his wedding? Come on, he'd look like an idiot. So even if a guy wants to be married to you, the ceremony is still going to feel a lot like spending a day looking like a dork.

Face it, ladies—at your wedding, *you* are the badass. He looks and feels like the accessory. That's how the guy has appeared at every wedding I've ever been at. (That guy up there doesn't look like he feels like a ninja or a Jedi or anything of the kind. He looks like he's at his First Communion in his big-boy clothes.)

Also, remember that men see things for what they *do*. A wedding is all about what it *means*. So that ceremony is always going to make more sense to you than it is to him. What does a wedding ceremony *do*? For the guy, it forces him to get dressed up in uncomfortable clothes and parades him around in front of people.

Does this mean that he doesn't want to be with you? Nope. Does it mean he doesn't want to marry you? Not that either. All it means is that you'll both be much happier if you acknowledge (if you don't know it already) that your wedding day is about you getting what you, as the woman, want. Well, you and any maiden aunts you have who love to go to weddings. (We'll talk about how to get your man psyched about the wedding a little later.)

MYTH: If I Contact Him after a Date, I Might Scare Him Off.

FACT: Unless you are dating a small woodland creature or someone with a serious anxiety disorder that makes him poop himself every time his phone rings, this is just flat-out not true, and it never, never happens. Ever. If he doesn't like you after you contact him, he didn't like you before, either.

I know, I know. You don't believe me. And so we'll talk more about this one in Chapter 4, "First Date Dos and Don'ts."

MYTH: I Shouldn't Have to Tell Him What I'm Thinking.

FACT: You only have to tell him what you're thinking if you want him to ever, *ever* know.

Men want badly to read your minds. We really, really do. I swear, if we could gain the power to read your mind by cutting off a randomly selected toe, we would all give it serious consideration. But we never will. (And to save you some time, I already looked into it, okay? No one is offering that trade.)

Let's take flowers, for example. If you were paying attention to the "What it DOES vs. What it MEANS" section in Chapter 1, you can guess how most men feel about flowers. They don't really register for men, because they don't *do* anything, so most men sort of forget they exist. But if, like many women, you enjoy getting flowers from time to time for no reason at all (i.e., when he's not in big, big trouble—even the dopiest of men knows to buy them for you then), do you know how you're going to get them? No, no, not by giving him flowers for no reason and hoping he gets the hint. He doesn't want flowers. How is giving him something that he does *not* want going to train him to give you something that you *do* want? You get your flowers by telling your man exactly that information—if he knows what you want (elk), he'll get it (stab).

I can hear you. I know, I know. You don't *want* to tell him. You want him to just *know*.

I don't know what to tell you. Date the Amazing Kreskin.

MYTH: I Can Change Him, and He'll Be So Much Happier.

FACT: Not unless you're talking about his diaper (in which case, you are very correct). This isn't Barbies, okay? He's not a Ken Doll. You don't want Ken, anyway. First of all, you want a guy you really want—as opposed to a guy you don't want but are pretty sure you can somehow Frankenstein into a guy you want. (Don't you have enough to do throughout the day?)

And second, Ken has no genitals. It's just smooth down there. Who needs that?

Myth: Men Are Like Dogs
Fact: They Really Are

- Dogs Cannot Read Your Thoughts. When you're mad at your dog, he has no idea why. He just knows you're mad because you're using your "bad doggie" voice. Exact same thing with us. The difference with us is that you can tell us why you're upset. You know, if you wanted to throw us a bone. (A figurative one for men. Dogs would prefer the actual thing.)
- Dogs Cannot Direct Their Attention. If there's a squirrel in your yard, the dog is going to go nuts. What are you going to do, tell him to be reasonable? It's the same thing with men and, say, cleavage. If it's around, we can't help but pay attention to it.*
- Dogs Pay an Inordinate Amount of Attention to Their Own Crotches and to the Crotches of Others. Don't know what this one is about, but hey, just be grateful we're not also obsessed with eating our own poop.

---

* And even if we're talking about a highly trained dog—one that can sit there for twenty minutes with a biscuit on his nose until you say, "Okay!"—even that dog is only thinking about the moment when you'll finally let him eat the thing. Some helpful advice, though: I would not recommend training your man in this fashion. If you try to balance some other woman's cleavage on your boyfriend's nose, someone's liable to get hurt.

FEELINGS: AN EXPOSÉ

Men and women seem to have some very different attitudes, training, and behaviors about feelings. There are several misconceptions that I've heard from many women. Let's go through a few of the major ones.

MYTH: Men Are Afraid to Talk about Their Feelings.

FACT: Men are afraid when you ask them to talk about their feelings—because they have no idea what you want them to be feeling in that moment.

I'm not saying men don't have feelings. I'm sure we must. But if you ask me, "What are you feeling right now?"— frankly, I'm stumped. Not because there was nothing going on with me just then, but because I know that if I say, "I was just...thinking that if I try XYZ strategy in my new video game, I could get past that really hard place where the big alien keeps smooshing me," I'm going to be in big, big trouble.

Here's what it is. Men don't usually spend much time paying attention to how we're feeling unless we're really angry, really scared, or really hungry. And we know that women do pay attention to that kind of thing. You know exactly how you're feeling. We're afraid that you not only know how *you* are feeling, but you probably know how *we* are feeling—and we're going to get it wrong, and you're going to get mad.

If you want to know how a man is feeling, understand that you are doing the equivalent of asking your dog if he wants to go skiing. He'll know you want some damn thing from him, but for the life of him, he won't know what it is. He'll *want* to know what it is. Badly. But since he's only too aware that he doesn't understand what you want, he's just trying to come up with anything that might keep you from getting mad. Because you have access to all the treats he likes.

This brings us to a "companion myth":

MYTH: Because They Can't Talk about Their Feelings, Men Aren't in Touch with Them.

FACT: Men are more in touch with their feelings than women are.

What? *Men?* More in touch with their feelings than women—the black-belt feelings experts? Yes. Yes, I believe that men are far less capable of denying their emotions than women are. Men get a bum rap about their emotions.

Women seem to have fallen under the impression that men aren't in touch with their feelings, because we are so unwilling to talk about them. You couldn't be more wrong.

Stay with me. Given that we are extremely incapable of discussing our feelings, how can I say that men are 100 percent in touch with them?

Here's how. Even when we can't talk about what we're feeling, even when we say the exact opposite of what we're feeling, even when we haven't the slightest idea what we are feeling, men are always *behaving* in strict accordance with what we're feeling. (Ahem. Golden Rule. *Again.*) Remember that dog you were so good at imagining? It's like that. We can't help it.

What this means to you, the common man-dater, is that
even though he might not be able to talk to you about his
feelings, you'll always be able to see what they are.

MYTH: Men Would Be Better Off If They Could Talk about Their Feelings.

FACT: Men are mostly okay with how often we talk about
our feelings. Women certainly do seem to want us to do it
more, though.

I don't know what this one is all about. Most men see little
reason to talk about their feelings, even if they were to spend
time thinking about them.

Sure, we don't talk about them. But that only means that
we don't think about feelings consciously. Remember, men
secretly think they might be called upon at any moment to
stop the Nazis from finding the Lost Ark of the Covenant
and ruling the world. How would thinking about our feelings help us in that situation? There's a giant boulder rolling
after us; a guy's saying, "Throw me the idol, I throw you the
wheep." How is it going to help us to know that we're feeling
insecure and vulnerable right then?

*But why can't you just tell us the truth about
whatever you're really feeling?*

...I hear you saying, in fancy ladyscript.

Two reasons:

1. He doesn't really know or care about the truth, and

2. You don't want the truth.

When you ask what's on a man's mind, he knows that there are only a couple of acceptable answers. And he had better be thinking one of them. He might be 100 percent crazy about you and *still* be thinking about his taxes while he's out on a date with you. He knows he can't say *that*.

My advice? Stop asking for this one. Be honest for a second—most often when a woman wants to know what a man is thinking or feeling, she's fishing for a compliment, right? If you want a compliment, just ask him for one directly. And don't be afraid to tell us what kind of compliment, either. ("You there. Isn't my new haircut the kind of thing that a boyfriend might want to say looks really cute? It's exactly that kind of thing, isn't it?") My girlfriend does this all the time, and it works like a dream. Trust me, he'll be only too thrilled to spear the holy hell out of the exact elk that you need speared. Then everybody's happy, and nobody has to get yelled at.

MYTH: If a Man Doesn't Cry, It Means He's Not in Touch with His Feelings.

FACT: If a man doesn't cry, it means that he is not experiencing an emergency situation.

Okay, imagine you're at your job, and one of the women who works with you starts crying right in the middle of the salmon cannery assembly line (hey, I don't know where you work). What would happen? Mmm, nothing much. Everyone would wonder what was wrong, and someone would probably ask her, and it would work itself out in a matter of minutes.

Okay, now imagine one of the men you work with just bursting into tears at work. What would happen? The whole place would go nuts. Everyone would think that something must really be wrong, or else Balthazar (I don't know who you work with, either) wouldn't be crying in public. And everyone would talk about it for years.

For whatever reason, we just don't get to cry in front of people very often. And we don't really want to. Look, until men can find some big upside to crying (i.e., what it *does*), we're not going to do it very often. Personally, unless I've just been dumped (or seen the last twenty minutes of *The Iron Giant*), it just doesn't come up.

It's the "men who don't cry, don't feel" myth that leads some women to this next one:

MYTH: Men Don't Get Brokenhearted in the Same Way That Women Do.

FACT: We most certainly do, but it might not look like you expect it to.

A woman wrote to me once wondering if men are incapable of feeling brokenhearted after a breakup. This came up because she heard that her ex was out trying to get laid only days after they had split up. She was understandably hurt that he was already looking for someone else, but I can tell you that there's no reason to think that guy wasn't absolutely crushed. But you're never, never going to see it.

First of all, we've already talked about crying. So you're not likely to see any visible signs that he's an emotional wreck. Not in public. Not unless something really heavy just rolled over his toes.

But what about the "getting laid" part? How could he possibly be ready to be with another woman already? Well, that's the problem right there—you think he needs to get "ready" to be with another woman. I assure you, he's been "ready" since he was, oh, twelve years old. Whatever woman he can corral into his bed has nothing to do with his vulnerable emotional state. The fact is, he is probably out looking to get laid to *avoid* vulnerability.

I know, I know. Weird and strange, right? Well, no worries. That's what the next chapter is all about.

See? As promised, we've cracked open a ton of the myths about men, and we didn't even have to pretend that the sun was the chariot of Apollo or anything.

Next, we'll tackle myths, misunderstandings, and foolishness about a topic so private, so smoking hot-t-t, so potentially embarrassing, that it deserves its very own chapter. I give you...

the notorious s.e.x., or abandon
hope all ye who enter here

Many of the myths that women seem to believe about
men revolve around the fundamental differences in
how the two genders experience sex. (Quick review: The two
genders are "men" and "women." Just making sure that you
didn't get lost in all this relationship jargon.) So let's talk
about that. Sex, I mean. Ahem… let's do that. Er… is it
warm in here?

Okay, clearly I'm a little uncomfortable with the subject,
as I am from Connecticut, where we pretend that such things
never happen, lest we blush so hard we have to be taken to the
emergency room. So you can only imagine how embarrassed
I am to write about… ahem… sex.

And clearly I'm not the only one who's a little nervous
about this subject. Take, for example, the time-honored sex
lesson, wherein some adult coughs and blushes his or her way
through a thirty-second explanation of where babies come
from. If you ever had any doubt about our society's discom-
fort with the idea of sex, think about the image they chose:

THE BIRDS AND THE BEES

Uh… wha? Even granting the premise that children should
be talking about animal sex at all, um, could we have come up

with two animals with *less* obvious genitalia? I'm in my late thirties, and I haven't the slightest notion of what's going on below the belt for either species.

I do know that both of them lay eggs. So far, not helpful. And bees live in some weird configuration in which there's one female for the whole society. And before we start thinking that this might be somehow fun for her, it's not like she gets a room filled with Brad Pitt and George Clooney. It's just bees. Not that she's anyone to judge, being a bee herself. Okay, now that I think about it, that seems okay. But still, it's not going to help any of us primates get laid, so why are we even talking about it?

Anyway, in this section of the book, we'll talk about some of the things that women seem to believe about men regarding sex, and we'll explore just what the truth is about the whole thing. It seems to me that there are four distinct areas of the male mind that we need to cover:

1. Thinking about sex (also known as the "vast majority of the time")

2. Pursuing sex (not quite as much of the time as in number one, but still a lot)

3. During sex (not nearly as much of the time as numbers one or two... for me, at least)

4. After sex (that ten-minute period before we head right back to number one)

By the time we get through here, you're going to know way, way more about men than maybe you even wanted to.

(Get ready: In the area of sex, we're far more different from each other than you probably imagine.)

THINKING ABOUT SEX, OR EXCELLENT REASONS NEVER TO ASK A MAN WHAT HE'S THINKING

Okay, from what I'm told, this is one area in which men and women aren't even remotely similar. And no matter what you think we're thinking, it's probably... worse. Think of what is sometimes considered the cheapest, trashiest version of the female fantasy—the romance novel. A romance novel is related to a male fantasy in the way that a nice cup of coffee is related to crystal meth.

The Porn Fascination

Porn has been involved in *every* technological leap we've ever made—and probably within about ten minutes of each leap, going all the way back to pioneer times. Consider:

- Computers = computer porn

- VCRs = VHS porn

- Film = film porn

- Telephone = phone sex

- Telegraph = I'm sure that ten minutes after this was invented, there was a guy working the telegraph with one hand and whacking off with the other.

What comes next? My guess: virtual reality. As soon as this technology is invented, society is in big, big trouble. Seriously. They have this on *Star Trek* where you can go into a room and experience full-body holograms of whatever you ask for. Look, as soon as that happens, there will be no starships, no lasers, no war, no industry, and no society. The day that a guy can press a button and have sex with Jessica Alba/Simpson/ Biel is the day that no one ever goes to work again.

Why do we always make porn out of technology? Because the guys who make brilliant leaps in technology aren't seeing the business end of a boob very often. Think of the guys who invented the Internet. (No, not Al Gore—the other guys.) About ten seconds after they came up with it, I'm sure they were working on ways to meet women, real or otherwise. It's just the natural way.

So how do you, the girlfriend/wife/what-have-you, deal with this obsession? Porn is not *so* different from what the two of you are supposed to be doing together… and ain't no way you're doing… *that.*

No worries. A real man doesn't expect you to. This is just his fantasy world. Hold on, don't get disgusted. Remember male sexual fantasies? Remember how I told you they weren't like your fantasies? Yeah, here's what I was talking about. A man does not watch porn like an athlete watching game tape, looking for tips and planning out his next move. (Well, a smart man doesn't do that, anyway.)

In other words, we don't have fantasies about this stuff thinking that it might actually happen. (The things that we are allowed to actually do, we just do. Why fantasize about… reality?)

I know you want him to fantasize differently. I know, I know. But he doesn't. The good news is it shouldn't matter.

I know that there are men who are "addicted" to porn, but that's a different thing. If we're talking about your average man with your average porn fascination? No worries: We do not expect or need you to like it.

And if he does want you to get into watching and/or emulating porn with him, there's nothing wrong with saying, "Listen, that stuff doesn't do it for me, okay? It's not my thing." Just make sure you follow that up with, "But you know what does do it for me…?" I think you'll find that this is one of those areas in which men can be excellent listeners.

Fake Biology Break

Okay, if I may, I'd like to pause for a moment and talk science. Given that I went to an arts school where my math *and* science requirements were fulfilled by taking a nutrition class taught by a fat person, feel free to take this "science" with a grain of salt. (But only a grain, because, as I recall from that class, sodium is bad for you. Or maybe it was good for you. Hard to remember when the teacher once listed a doughnut as a part of a healthy breakfast. Seriously.)

Here's the issue for men. We are biologically predetermined to be the aggressors in sex, because we can make as many babies as there are vaginas to put them in. Women can only make one baby at a time. Or two, in my sister's case. Actually, wasn't there somebody on the news who had, like, eleven at once? Look, let's not get all hung up on the numbers. No matter how many babies there are, they still only have one place to hang around in until they're born, is my point. And for good or ill, men don't have that physical restriction.

Now, this doesn't mean that all men need to do something about that fact, but on a purely physical level, men are only limited by (a) the hours in the day, and (b) our ability to convince you ladies to let us do sex unto you.

So since our brains are constantly on the lookout for potential vacation spots for our penises, men are biologically trained to constantly be on the lookout for women who fit one of two criteria:

1. They are totally smoking hot, or

2. They might be willing to have sex with us.

Preferably both at the same time.

It's not personal. Your man—yes, *your* man—wants to have sex with every woman he sees. Not necessarily in an active way. He's not "after" her. He doesn't care about her. Doesn't have to. His brain and body are just alerting him to the fact that she exists and is potentially available for sex. And if a woman wants to have sex with him, this puts the male body/mind on full alert. Why? Because that's one of those two criteria—it's battle stations! "Alert! Alert! Sex is 100 percent available! DEFCON 1! Other alert-type noises!"

This is where we see the big misunderstanding: "How can he want to have sex with her? She's an idiot!" Well, maybe so, but she is either a hot idiot or a willing idiot. Biologically speaking, we are not designed to let those things slip our attention. In a very real way, that is what male attention is for. (That and hooking up home-theater equipment.) The reason why he wants to have sex with her is that she exists and is, in some way, attractive. That's the beginning and end of it.

Note that men don't generally attach much significance to our sexual fantasies. Sometimes we don't even really notice that we've had one. It's just our brain's way of saying "hi."

As in, "Oh, we're looking at a woman. Okay, let's run that through the simulator. Yep. That's what sex with *her* might be like. Okay, let's move on with our day."

Such a Near Miss

How many times have you seen a Civil War–themed romance novel cover on which some unrealistically buxom Confederate war widow is leaning back, breathless, on her veranda, as a wounded, shirtless Union soldier is ravaging her?

Okay, but then you also have men—actual living men—who are putting on that very same outfit and reenacting great battles of that same Civil War with like-minded idiots. If these men weren't such dorks, and if the women who are reading those romance novels would get rid of some of their cats, and if they would both take a few spinning classes, they could reenact both parts together! The guys would get to run around, pretending to shoot their dork friends, and then go home and bang the holy living hell out of their costumed lady friend on the veranda. It's a win-win. Such a shame. Ah, well.

Here's an image for you. Think of a man's conscious mind as being not unlike your own. And then, imagine the part of his brain that's in charge of sexual fantasies sitting off to the side, not unlike a crack-addicted chipmunk flipping through seven hundred channels of homemade porn featuring every woman he's ever thought of for longer than, say, a nanosecond. Lots of times we're not even paying any attention. It's like cleaning the house with the TV on.

I know that sounds gross, but it's true. And if it's any consolation, it's probably a lot grosser than you're picturing.

Just thank whatever god(s) you worship for your inability to visualize it accurately.

And no matter how disgusted with us you become, you just don't know the half of it. Which brings us to our first sex myth:

MYTH: Men Only Ever Think about Sex.

FACT: However much time you think we spend on this, well, it's probably more.

When you roll your eyes and say that men are only ever thinking about sex, see, you think you mean that figuratively, but I'm telling you that men are *literally always* thinking about sex.

I have occasionally heard one or another woman—disgusted with some dude's behavior—say something along the lines of, "I swear, half the time he's only thinking about sex!"

I always wonder what in the holy hell she imagines he's thinking about the other half of the time??! Are you kidding me? I couldn't possibly fill up *half my day* thinking about... see? I can't even think of stuff that would occupy one out of every two thoughts, let alone actually think those thoughts. I think about video games, computers, and giant televisions a lot, and that's still got to cover at most maybe 10 percent of the time.

Now, that doesn't mean that men are *only* thinking about sex. It just means that there is always some little piece of our brains thinking about sex. In the background, I'm saying. Just like the way that no matter whom you're talking to, you are subconsciously aware of every pair of shoes in the room and whether or not you think those shoes are cute. It's called "multitasking," people.

Sex with whom?

Anybody. Everybody. You. Your friends, your sister, people we saw on the train. Celebrities, coworkers, or that time we saw half a boob across a crowded room and pieced her together into a whole woman.

It's not exactly "thinking," per se. It's just our mental filing system doing its thing: "Okay. Let's put her in the *dopey but gorgeous* section, and cross-file her under *possible threesomes with Jessica Alba.*"(Sorry, sorry. I'm so, so sorry.)

Yes. Every man who sees you is thinking, however briefly, about having sex with you.

Please re-read that sentence.

No, read it again.

See, I think you skimmed it and reinterpreted it to mean that "a lot" of the "disgusting" men are thinking about having sex with "some women" and "some of the time." No, I'm talking about *you*, and I'm talking about *all* of us, even the nice guys.

You know what, I don't think you're ever going to believe me on this one. And it's for the best. I think the fact that you can't believe that I'm serious right now is Mother Nature's little way of ensuring that you'll let us have sex with you enough times to keep the species going.*

A Difficult Truth about Men and Masturbation

Let me tell you something disturbing. This is a horrible thing to know about all of the men in your life. Ready to learn something just terrible? Here we go.

---

* I hate to think that sex might or might not result in children. It would be as if every time you ate ice cream, there was a chance that you might burst into flames. Such a cruel trick played by Mother Nature. Personally, I think you should have to fill out some paperwork or something to get a kid and just let sex be fun. But no one in charge really cares that I think that.

Every man in your life thought about you while whacking off at least one time. Maybe only for a couple of seconds. But they did it. Yep. Every man you know and many you don't. (No, not your relatives, sickos. But probably all of their friends.)

I'm not suggesting that each of them spent a lot of time on you. The duration of the male sexual fantasy is counted in milliseconds—as in, somewhere between one and five seconds is plenty, and then the aforementioned crack-addicted chipmunk switches channels. But trust me, you were in there somewhere. Maybe not every time, maybe not often, maybe not for very long. But it happened.

If it helps in any way, these guys were picturing you having a fantastic time. Or both of you, as the case may be.

Knowing this, you should be aware of what happens when you are in public. If you're attempting to be sexy out there, you might attract the attention of your targeted man, but it's not exactly a surgical strike. You are also going to hit every other man in sight. And you don't get to decide which one of them gets the fantasy. We're all getting it.

And for what it's worth, we really appreciate it.

Given that, you're probably ready to debunk this next one without my help, right?

MYTH: When a Man Likes a Woman, He Only Fantasizes about Her.

FACT: It doesn't matter who a man wants/likes/loves, he is going to fantasize about her, her friends, her sister, maybe her mom if she's hot, his ninth-grade Spanish teacher, that girl on the train, and that honey he saw in college that time where he didn't quite get a good look at the whole woman.

This dovetails neatly into the next one:

MYTH: My Boyfriend Isn't Like That.

FACT: Oh, yes, he is. And it's fine, I swear.

Look, even I'm like this, and I'm *nice*. I love my girlfriend; I brush my teeth several times a day; and I do my taxes on time. I'm about as *nice-enough-to-introduce-to-your-grandmother* a guy as you're likely to meet (as embarrassing as that may be), and yet the contents of my brain at any given moment would probably shock and offend Courtney Love, if only she could stay awake long enough for someone to explain them to her.

Fantasy: Girl-on-Girl Action

In October 2007, scientists figured out how to get female worms to be attracted to other female worms instead of males.

Let's put aside, for a moment, any questions about whether a worm has a lot of choices anyway. Look, you're a worm: everybody's covered in dirt; everybody looks really weird yet indistinguishable from each other; nobody's got any money. It's like living in New York City, just without arms, legs, or an iPod.

But in terms of application of this study, the scientist cautions anyone who thinks that this is going to unravel the mysteries of human sexuality. "A human's brain is much more complex than a worm's brain," he* said. Yeah, right. Says the man spending his days trying to teach worms to switch-hit.

The point is this: Every man who read about this wondered if they had an experimental version of the treatment that he could try out on his girlfriend.

We aren't 100 percent sure why we want you ladies to bat for the other team at least once. Lots of women think

---

* The scientist in question, Dr. Erik Jorgensen, director of the Brain Institute at the University of Utah, has been awarded the prestigious Only Footnote in this Entire Book to Contain Actual Research Award. Congratulations, Doc!

it's because men like the idea of being the center of attention in bed, and they might not be wrong there.

Personally, I think the whole girl-on-girl fantasy comes from this: When two women are having sex, a woman made the first move, which is hot. She almost had to have, right? (I mean, unless the two of them got a phone call from a third party asking them to do each other or something, which...does that ever happen?)

PURSUING SEX, OR AS IF HIS HAIR IS ON FIRE

Okay, is everybody still with me? Anybody decide to join a nunnery or sign up for a solo space mission or anything? Good. The worst is over.

Now we get into what happens with the male mind as he is actually going after sex. Remember, this isn't necessarily in any way related to whom he's fantasizing about. This is when it's for real.

Let's start with maybe the biggest mistake a woman can make in trying to read a man's intention:

MYTH: If a Man Wants to Have Sex with You, It Must Mean That He Likes You.

FACT: If a man wants to have sex with you, it means that he is alive and capable of imagining having sex with you. There is no relationship between a man wanting to have sex with you and a man liking you.

Now, I'm not saying that if a man wants to have sex with you he *doesn't* like you. He might—who knows? But the sexual desire by itself isn't an indicator of anything. After all, that's only one of the Two Big Questions.* It's never enough information.**

To put this another way, all men want to have sex with you, but only some of them want to date you. It's like a pyramid:

Men
who want to
spend the rest of
their life with you.

Men who want to date
you for a while.

Men who have pictured having sex
with you. (Every man who has ever seen
you. Seriously. Everybody. Even that time
when you had the flu and were wandering
around your dorm in your sweatpants.)

---

* See page 10. You know, in case you've already forgotten them.
** Think of it like buying shoes. You'd never judge shoes just because they looked great. You'd need to know that they were super comfortable as well, or you'd never even consider them, right? Okay, bad example.

Okay, I think you're probably getting the hang of it now, so let's look at a tricky one:

MYTH: There Are Two Types of Men: The Kind Who Only Want Sex and the Kind Who Want Relationships.

FACT: All men have two types of *interest:* either he wants to have sex with you *and* date you, or he wants to have sex with you *and not* date you.

Sounds similar, but it's totally different. See, it's not that there are the "nice" guys out there who will always want a relationship and then there are the jerks who are only after sex. Sex and dating are not related in quite that way for us. Nice guys or jerks, we all unconsciously categorize women in one of those two ways. Either it's sex *and* relationship, or it's sex *and not* relationship.

So if a guy only wants to sleep with you, that's how he sees *you* specifically—not necessarily how he sees all women. And a different guy might want to date you specifically, even though he thinks of your friends as people to sleep with. (And yes, the guy who wants to date you does think about sleeping with your friends. And so does the guy who doesn't want to date you. It's very equal-opportunity.)

So we know that men fantasize about all women, but what about going after them?

MYTH: Men Only Go After Women with Perfect Bodies.

FACT: Men not only want women with perfect bodies; we want their friends, their sisters, maybe their moms, their ninth-grade Spanish teacher... you get the idea.

Here's a problem in our society: The pervasive attitude among American women is that they are fatter/skinnier/taller/ shorter than they should be, that they are being compared to models with unrealistically perfect bodies, that men are only interested in women of that type, and if they are not perfect, men will not pay attention to them.*

I am here to help and/or be funny in the process. Maybe not in that order.

First, I am not going to lie to you. Yes, we all really do want to have sex with the models with the perfect bodies and the big, fake boobs and all of that. We want it all the time. I want it right now. In fact, every time I see one of those women, yes, I think about having sex with her. And even when I don't see one of them. That's what memory is for.

Women know this and think, "Well, how do the rest of us stand a chance?"

Here's how you stand a chance. We are not looking for ONE woman. We are looking for zillions of women. And we would love for you to be one of them.

Okay, that didn't really come out right.

What I am getting at is this. Most men do not really have a "type," any more than professional wrestling has rules. It's more of a "hey, whatever works" kind of philosophy. We look at *all* women.

Listen, I know how women often complain that men are only into appearance, and they always date younger women, etcetera, etcetera. And how women are more than happy to date older men, etcetera, etcetera.

---

* Let's forget for a moment that many of the women we're talking about (supermodels, etc.) only appear in magazines that men never read.

Fine, but let's not pretend that women are into these "older men" because of the content of their characters. Look at these older men that women want to sleep with. Who are these men? Sean Connery? Harrison Ford?

Probably just a coincidence that they are powerful, famous, and rich. I'm sure that if Sean Connery worked as a greeter at Wal-Mart to supplement his $300-a-month Social Security check, you'd still be after him, right?

Guys don't *only* care about a woman's looks any more than a woman *only* cares about a man's bank account. (Or his guitar playing, if she's under twenty-five or so.)*

To get back to the original myth, men do not "only" want to have sex with *any* body type, age, or anything else. We entertain every possibility.

History Break: Sex and the Twentieth Century
Lots of the last century has been interpreted** with metaphors of male sexuality. If you don't mind hearing about penises as they relate to foreign policy, read on!

World War II

This was in the height of the classic American home, in which the man did X and the woman did Y. And when somebody came into your backyard and stomped all over your Pearl Harbor, well, it was a man's job to go out there and sock someone in the nose.

---

* The reason why the May/December relationships play out how they usually do is probably financial. If there is a couple who has a major difference in age, the older one is, generally speaking, the one with the money. And the younger one is the one with the looks. And yes, given a choice between two women—even complete moron women, let's say—most men are likely to go for the moron with the hot body rather than the moron with the huge bank account. I'll give you that one.

** By zillions of stand-up comics, strict Freudians, and militant feminists. Maybe the only metaphor in history ever to have been made by all three groups simultaneously. That's got to count for something.

Wars are often described in sexual terms. One man gets a little too big of a "war boner," and he swings it in the direction of some other man who doesn't like how big it is. So the second man gets HIS war boner together, and they swing them around at each other until one of them gives up or is dead.

If that sounds a little creepy, well, it is.

Cold War

This was another prime example of the "hey, get that boner out of that country!" kind of thinking. Russia kept poking its peter into various nations around it; we started pushing our pee-pee into all kinds of places around us. Neither of us liked how well the other one seemed to be doing with the lady countries. So we attempted to "nation cockblock" each other as best we could. Eventually, we won because they ran out of money. Which is totally a penis victory in the modern world. If a Porsche is an extension of the penis, how much more so is cold, hard cash?

Vietnam

As it has been said many times, the big fear was that we would "pull out." This was an example where the male ego could not take the fact that we simply could not give this country a war climax. So we just kept pumping away while North Vietnam pretended not to yawn and look at the clock.

Meanwhile, the Communists were fooling around with North Vietnam behind closed doors, and everyone knew it. We just could not let them get away with getting *our* woman country off.

By the way, this is exactly why those Vietnam veterans got so little respect back then. They somehow were blamed for not bringing North Vietnam to orgasm. (As it turns out, we are now hearing that that country had never even had one in the first place.)

It was during this time they invented THE PILL, which meant that women could fool around if they wanted to. And they suddenly realized that maybe they *did* want to. Before that, it was sort of about doing whatever your tweed-jacketed man wanted. Now, suddenly, a woman could go out there and say, "Do I want to have sex? You know, I think that yeah, I actually do," and a line of confused and aroused men would form.

DURING SEX, OR WHEN FANTASY (OCCASIONALLY) BECOMES REALITY

Okay, here we are. Doin' it, going all the way, hitting a homer, and other nicknames we haven't used since we were eleven. There are definitely some major differences between men and women here as well.*

And we'll start with one that no amount of trashy airport reading can help you with. This is the single most common Google search that brings people to my website—and by a *wide* margin:

How to Drive Your Man Wild in Bed!!!

Look, no one's going to stop you from doing that weird ice-cube-in-the-mouth trick they always want to teach you in

---

* I won't get into our physiological differences, because, let's face it, if you don't know what they are, you're probably too young to read this book. Well, either that or you've never spoken to another human, in which case, I can't imagine how you learned to read. Or found a bookstore.

magazines. Knock yourself out. But you really don't need to be sweating this issue. Just follow these simple steps, and I guarantee you will drive him wild in bed:

- *Be Alive:* Now, don't skip this one just because it's easy. In fact, if you only follow one rule, this one should be it.

- *Go to Bed with Him:* Also crucial.

- *Make Sure You're Having Fun:* This helps in two ways. First, you'll be having fun, which is, you know, fun. And second, when you have a good time in bed, it helps us feel like a badass, fulfilling the Jack Bauer Principle. Plus, again, you'll be having fun. Nobody wants to be in bed with someone who is acting like they're on a trip to the dentist. Not unless your dentist is a lot more fun than mine.

That's it. That's the whole list. The danger of those magazine checklists is that they're checklists. As in, they're impersonal. Some weird checklist of advanced humping techniques might just make him wonder what other guys have been receiving this royal treatment. Most men like to think they're the only man in the world that you'd do this with. (I know, I know. I already said how we're picturing ourselves with a zillion other women. But that's us. We don't want *you* thinking like that.)

This brings us to another one of the most common questions that I get from women:

What if he fantasizes about other women when we're doin' it?

Well, here's another area in which this is probably a lot worse than you think. But it's also better, I promise.

Okay, here goes. This is not a "what if." All men do this. All of us. And just please don't ask whom we're fantasizing about, okay? You already know the answer: everybody. I know. It's awful. But before you start sharpening various knives, forks, and tongs with which to stab, poke, and… tong… your dude, I think it's time for a definition:

Male Fidelity: Defined

A woman recently wrote to me with a question about whether it was normal for a man to fantasize about other women—celebrities, ex-girlfriends, etc.—during sex, and if so, how is that not infidelity?

Here's how. For a man, fidelity and fantasy are very, very different. For us, sexual fantasies are involuntary. Cheating is a choice.

To put it another way, what fidelity does *not* mean is that he'll never think about anyone else ever again. He couldn't do that if he tried. (And he's not gonna try.) Fidelity means that even though he absolutely does fantasize about all other women on the planet Earth (and that restriction is only there because that's the only planet that has any women on it), he chooses to be with you and only you.

Now, this doesn't mean you have to stand for *hearing* about it. When this woman told me her man was fantasizing about "ex-girlfriends" during sex, my initial thought was, "Is there actually a man that moronic out there? Why in the world did he actually *tell* her that?" And the answer is that he messed up a little. These little "moron movies" are his business, and as long as they don't mean anything, they should remain his business.

And you are well within your rights as a woman to say, "Hey, listen, whatever happens inside your warped, little mind is your business, okay? I'm not crazy about the idea, but I can't fight biology. But if I ever, ever actually hear about it again—oh, boy, is there going to be big friggin' trouble. In your brain, sure, anything goes. Out here, it's all about *me*, please. Okay?"

I know that I've made the male fantasy sound like pretty much the most horrific thing you've ever imagined. And if it were on your TV right now, wow, it sure would be. You thought Janet Jackson's nipple got angry letters. If one of these things ever aired, somebody would be going to jail. But just know these fantasies can't hurt you. They don't tell you anything about his commitment or anything else.

And now, yet another very, very common web search that brings womenfolk my way:

How to Ask for What You Want in Bed

So what if he's not, uh, driving you wild in bed? How do you approach it so everybody can get exactly what they're after? It sort of depends on what kind of wrong he is:

- *New Cop on the Force:* You might be with someone who's inexperienced. His confidence is probably not there yet, and he's probably very, very aware that he's doing it all wrong. And he's probably terrified that you think that and doesn't want to bring it up. The key with this guy is encouragement. You want to guide him in the right direction and let him know that you're loving it when he does something well. The last thing you want to do is to make him feel like you think he's a rookie who is no good at this.

• *Thinks He's Great:* There are lots of dudes who really think they are total black belts in the sack. And let's face it, if this is like everything else in the freaking world, I'm guessing that there are probably a lot more guys who think they're great than actually are great. With this guy, it's still going to be about encouragement—but a different kind. And you might even have to... "lie." Just a little. As in, you might want to tell him, "Oh, I love it when you do XYZ!" even if he has never even approached doing that before. He might feel a little confused if he can't remember ever having done that before. But he'll still figure out a way to somehow give himself credit for having done it. And now that he knows how "great he was at it," he'll do it more.

• *Captain Checklist:* There are guys who think that they are great "technicians" in bed—i.e., they have various "moves" they do that they are sure "work." And they can't all be right. Don't encourage stuff that isn't working, or you'll get it all night long. With this guy, you want to make him feel like he's on the right track, but he just needs to calibrate his instruments to your specifications. And when he finally gets it right, make sure he knows about it.

- *Rebel without a Clue:* This is a guy who thinks that just by showing up, you're satisfied. (Why wouldn't you be? He sure is!) If he's going all "Speedy Gonzalez" on you, you might have to really reeducate him. This is a guy who doesn't realize that women are built differently than men. He's going to need to learn that he needs to do extra stuff to get you there—extra, as in beyond what needs to happen to get him there. Make suggestions of stuff you'd like to "try." And when it happens, let him see you love it. Rave about it. Communicate that whatever it was really worked.

- *Just Not Hitting It:* He's trying; he's listening; he's paying attention; and he's still just not clueing in. Same advice as the rookie. He's trying, but he needs some signposts along the way. Help him out. You'll get what you want, and he'll learn how to give it to you.

As you might have noticed, these all involve encouragement. Now, I've heard some women say, "Oh, why do I have to be protecting a man's precious ego in bed?" Well, you don't "have to" do anything. But... don't you like him? Don't you want him to feel good about himself and what he's doing? If not, hey, do whatever you want. But I'll tell you this much—if you're not getting what you want in the sack, well, you're definitely not going to get it by making him feel lousy about what he's doing. (That goes for in and out of bed, for that matter.)

AFTER SEX BUT BEFORE THINKING ABOUT SEX AGAIN, OR BLINK AND YOU'LL MISS IT

So there you are. In bed. Or on the floor. Hey, maybe you did it under your porch, for all I know. Wherever you did it, the point is that it's done. What's going on with him now?

I'm glad you asked me and not him.

MYTH: The Right Guy Will Want to Talk and Cuddle after Sex.

FACT: Maybe, maybe not.

For the answer to this one, it's time to go back to fake biology. It might help to think of the male brain as two entirely different characters.

1. *Sex Brain:* This is the guy who is in charge of securing the booty. You can think of him as a Viking named Karl. Or maybe Bjorn.

2. *Everything Else Brain:* This is the guy who picks up the dry cleaning, gets to work on time, watches Bigfoot shows on the Discovery Channel, etc.

When a man is trying to get a woman into bed, Sex Brain is very, very focused. That becomes *the* goal. However, the moment that the sex is finished, Sex Brain runs away laughing. Or he falls asleep. The point is, he's gone. Now, the Everything Else Brain can finally take a look around and see what's going on.

And yes, it's true that if the guy in question is not the right guy, it will likely be in this moment that he beats a hasty retreat. It's like in an old werewolf movie where the guy wakes up; his clothes are all torn up; he's covered in dirt and branches and twigs; and he wonders what in the holy hell happened.

But even some of the right guys aren't into snuggling and cooing sweet nothings in your ear. Why? I think it's the whole problem-solving thing that our brains are always working on. Once sex is over, well, that's one thing we can check off the list. Our brains are onto the next thing.

This is why it's not a great idea to ask an unsuspecting man, post sex, what he's thinking about. It's entirely possible that even a very loving man, right after sex, just thought of an awesome way to reorganize the garage.

Now that you've done it, what happens the next time he's with his idiot friends?

MYTH: When Men Get Together, They Talk about Sex All the Time.

FACT: Men talk about *women* all the time, but that isn't the same thing.

What men talk about is who they want to have sex with, who they *did* have sex with, who they were trying to have sex with, who wants to have sex with them, what happened the other night when they were trying to have sex with that girl and their so-called friend totally cockblocked them—but that girl totally wanted to have sex with them.

This, they talk about all the time. But that's not talking about sex. That's talking about getting sex. Men don't talk about the sex itself all that often. Not with me, anyway. (And if they're talking about it with each other when I'm not around, well, I appreciate their discretion in keeping me out of that loop.)

There are several reasons we don't talk about the actual sex that often. The main one for me is, I mean, where's the upside in telling my idiot friends in detail about some sexual experience I had? What—if I tell the story really, really well, I'll be in a room full of guys with boners, all imagining me having sex? It's just not optimal.

There is a slight exception. We will talk about sex if and only if the specifics demonstrate some superior level of conquest that we couldn't convey just by saying that we had sex. If it in some way flatters us that we got her to make that otter noise, we might bring it up. But it's all about me and what I was able to accomplish. We're not comparing notes.

Also, I definitely don't want my friend picturing the sex I'm having with a woman I actually care about. This part definitely goes back to caveman brain. Here's how it works. Back in the time of cave people, if you were turned on by my woman, I had to kill you with a stick.

So let's say that I am in a new-ish relationship with a woman, and I'm sitting around with my idiot friends (and I say that with much love, by the way, knowing full well that I, too, am an idiot friend to *my* friends). If any of them asks how it's going with the girl, my response will depend upon how I feel about her at that moment. The possible answers are

1. "Ugh. She's out of her freaking mind."
   Manslation: We will be going out for a little while, but you don't have to like her. This relationship is mostly about the fact that I'm allowed to have sex with her.

2. "Um… it's going really well. She's really cool."
   Manslation: Okay, I like this girl. So while I'm around, you now have to pretend you don't want to have sex with her, or I'll kill you.

Now, you might have noticed that I said that they would have to "pretend" they don't want to have sex with her. As we've established, every man wants to have sex with virtually every woman. So a man, of course, knows that his idiot friends want to do his girlfriend. He wants to, so why wouldn't they? However, if a guy is truly my friend, not only will he agree not to actually try to have sex with her but to pretend that he doesn't even think about it. This way, we can stay friends, and nobody needs to get smashed over the head with a folding chair.

WHEW… ANYBODY NEED A CIGARETTE?

That's it. That's everything you always wanted to know and many things that no one ever wanted to know. The bad news is that all of this is true. The good news is that the things that make us so incredibly different are exactly why sex is so fun.

And armed with this information, there's no reason you can't both be happy.

Oh, and if this chapter hasn't cured you of the urge to ask your man, "So what are you thinking about?" I don't know what will.

CHAPTER 4 ● first date dos and don'ts, or you're not wearing that, are you?

Everybody knows what a first date is. We've all seen *Happy Days*. A boy and a girl meet; they grow nauseous with desire and worry; one of them asks the other one if they'd like to go out on a date. And despite the fact that 99 percent of the time this ends in total disaster, we just keep right on doing it. Why? Well, this actually needs a little manslating.

Men and women have different fantasies about a first date.

Now, as we've already discussed, men and women have different fantasies about everything. So the first date is no exception. Here's the thing. I think you need to know what a man *does not* fantasize about so you can set your expectations.

"ROMANCE" EXPLAINED

For the male mind, "romance" is often a total mystery. We don't really get it. At all. We don't know what it's for (what it *does*—remember that part?)

For a woman, romance is often an essential part of the fantasy. A man comes through the door and sweeps her up into a whirlwind adventure, where he treats her like a princess and confesses things to her that no man has ever said—things that *he* has never revealed to any woman before. I'm not suggesting that every woman thinks this way or that they believe consciously that it's going to be like this. I'm just saying it's a template for the *kind* of thing that one's mind might flash on.

The main theme of this fantasy seems to be magic. As in, Cinderella-style magic: *my life was normal... until he came through my door.* It's what you dream about when you don't know someone very well.

I bring this up only to say that men don't fantasize about that. Ever. It's just not that fun or interesting for us. Men don't fantasize that our life becomes magical. We fantasize that we are Han Solo, or some version of a "cool guy." Our big fantasy is that you think we are the coolest guy in the world.

Now, of course, I'm just talking about what most people think before they know the person they're going out with. What most people ultimately want is to be in a real relationship in which they are both crazy about each other and love each other for exactly who they are.

But... we're talking about dating. Totally different thing. I'll break it down into sections and give you some dos and don'ts based on some manslations of what you may not know about male dating habits.

The sections are:

I. Getting the Date

II. Pre-Date

III. On the Date

IV. At the End of the Date

Before we get into these four sections (which, be honest, are pretty brilliant, aren't they?), we have to cover one of the big problems of modern dating: Where does one meet someone he/she might want to, you know, go on a date with?

Actually, this is easier now than ever before. Imagine you're a cavewoman. Where are you going to meet boys? Pretty much in your cave or no damn place at all. But now we've got all kinds of ways. Trouble is, most of them are terrible.

Bars

I know plenty of people who have met their person in a bar. Nothing wrong with that. It's nighttime; there's music; there's mood lighting; there's alcohol—what a great place to meet someone, right? Or at least a great place to meet someone who might be drinking.

Here's something important to realize, though. If you see a man hanging around in a bar (especially a dance club), there is only one manslation, and it is not "to dance." And it's probably not "to have a meaningful conversation," either. The manslation for a man at a dance club is *that's where he heard they were keeping all the vaginas.* (In fact, now that I say it, that's almost the only reason we leave the house at all.)

The Internet

Perhaps you've heard of it. It's that thing that lives inside your computer, where they put all the porn, cheap pharmaceuticals from across some border, and Nigerian banking schemes. And it's a hugely popular way to meet people with whom you might want to do the sex. The positives are that it's always available; you don't even have to leave your house to use it; and nobody knows who you are.

The negatives are… well… picture the majority of people for whom those "positives" are the big selling point? Right, exactly. I'm not discouraging you. I'm just letting you know that regardless of how rosy a picture some of these guys paint of themselves, the prince-to-frog ratio is pretty brutal. About the same as in, you know, the real world.

"Outside the Box" Ideas

Every once in a while, you read an article that tells you where you might want to meet up with dudes. The laundromat was a big one for a time (He does his laundry! Keeper!); so were bookstores, of course (Hey, at least he can read!), and hardware stores (He's so handy! What if your toilet breaks? He'll take care of it!).

Nothing wrong with any of these, but I have to tell you that the second there's an article saying that this or that place is an excellent place to meet men? Yep, you guessed it—all the players will swarm there, looking to cash in on all the newly hopeful women who read the article.

On my website, a woman once mused that there must be a bar somewhere that only nice guys went to. But I promise you, if there was a nice, clean bar called T.G.I. Considerates, by 9:00 p.m. it would be crowded to capacity with jerkoffs, and the nice guys wouldn't even be allowed in.

Meeting through Friends

This is widely considered the best method to meet someone. And it's hard to disagree—what are you going to do, meet someone through your enemies? Do you actually *have* enemies? Or perhaps an arch nemesis?

If I did have enemies, I surely wouldn't date based on their recommendations. That would probably be exactly what they'd want me to do. And they'd set me up with some psycho who… ah… now some of my old relationships make so much more sense…

Bottom line: It's always good to get a recommendation from a friend if you can manage it, along the lines of, "Hey, this guy is actually not insane." Great. Just make sure that your friend isn't insane. Kind of defeats the purpose of the recommendation.

So let's move ahead into the world of the First Date.

I. GETTING THE DATE

It seems to me that there are only two major ways to get a date: either he asks you out, or you ask him. I mean, I suppose that there must be other ways. Maybe he kidnaps you at gunpoint and decides he wants to take you out to the Olive Garden; maybe the two of you fall out of separate airplanes and land in the same movie theater. But these aren't situations that you really need to plan for.

For the most part, one of you has the idea that you want to go out on a date and asks the other one if they like that idea and want to do that. Simple, right? Everybody with me? Hello?

So with that said, let's focus on the two most likely possibilities:

Him Asking You Out—Old Faithful

If you want him to ask you out, here are some dos and
don'ts.

Do

- *Meet Him:* Failure to do this will almost certainly
  result in not going out on a date with him. He can't
  come to your house and find you. And if he can,
  he probably works for the NSA or the CIA, and
  he's been tapping your phone or something. Which,
  hey, whatever turns you on.

- *Talk to Him:* Again, you're likely going to have to
  do this at some point. I realize how terrifying this
  can be when you don't know somebody very well.
  But there's not too much to be done about it. I'm
  sorry.

- *Be Fun:* I know, now I'm just being prejudiced
  against the boring and intolerable. I get that. But
  nonetheless, you're far more likely to get him to ask
  you out if he is of the opinion that talking to you is
  enjoyable and being on a date with you will be even
  more enjoyable. It's just the way it goes.

- *Make Him Feel Welcome:* You'd be surprised how
  many times a woman will not behave as if she even
  wants him around. He may like to think of himself
  as a bad-assed ninja or Jedi who would never, never
  be too intimidated to ask a woman out and all, but
  if he feels like you're happy he's there, it might ease
  his mind about asking you out. You know, a little.

Don't

- *Play Hard to Get:* I'm not saying that you have to flop over backward for every guy. But there's been a lot of misinformation out there about how men love to chase women (which is true), and so women should become more "challenging" (which is… probably not true). The only problem with this is that there's a fine line between "playing hard to get" and "making him feel like a jerk for trying." Again, be nice, be fun, and make him feel like you're happy he's there.

- *Drop "Hints":* By this, all I mean is that you shouldn't assume that men have the slightest idea how to read your secret code. A woman wrote to me once complaining that her intended beau wasn't picking up on her hints. Know what the "hints" were? She mentioned one time that she wanted to see a certain movie, and then she pretty much ignored him. For six months. I'm not kidding. I defy Sherlock Holmes to find that clue.*

As frustrating as it may be, you should never underestimate a man's total ineptitude at picking up on hints.

- *Try to Be Somebody Else:* See, here's the downside of putting on an act to get someone to ask you out.

---

* You probably don't want to date Sherlock Holmes anyway. He was hooked on cocaine. Plus check out the hat. Your friends would never let you hear the end of it.

Firstly, you're not Meryl Streep. He's not fooled. So all he gets from this is that you're behaving strangely. Secondly, if you somehow DO manage to fool him, uh, what's going to happen later when you're not BS-ing him anymore?

You Asking Him Out—A Brave, New-ish World

Let's say that you like a guy and you want to ask *him* out. Pretty crazy, huh? Huh? Next thing, you're going to be picketing in Washington and signing petitions for the right to smoke on the Sabbath.

I'll put it another way. You're fine asking him out. You're well within your rights as a human and an American. Or as a Canadian. In Europe you need a writ. And in all other lands, please check your local ordinances.

Do (There's only one "do." It's a pretty simple operation.)

- *Actually Ask Him Out:* And by that I mean that you should ask him to go somewhere—and not as a pal or a coworker or a fellow marmot enthusiast or whatever. Ask him out on a date. Scary? Yes. But the alternative is far scarier: you'll actually be out on the date, and you'll have no idea if he knows that it's a date. I just peed a little at the thought. Please be clear, as if you're speaking to a small child who needs everything laid out very clearly.

Don't

- *Worry That This Makes You Look Desperate:* It does not. This is the number one fear that women have

about asking a man out. How do I know that? I
hear this one all the time: "I don't want to look desperate." You know what makes you look desperate?
When you want to ask a man out, but instead you
spend all your time trying to drop wilder and wilder
hints that he should ask you out. Relax.

- *Pretend You're Not Nervous:* Why do that? So he
  thinks that he's in no way special and that you ask
  guys out every ten minutes? It's good to be nervous.
  It makes him feel good knowing that you like him
  enough to get a little freaked. It helps him feel like
  a badass. Which is nice because he might be exactly
  as nervous as you are.

- *Chicken Out:* Guys ask women out all the time. Yes,
  it's terrifying. That awful barfy sensation in your gut?
  Yeah, that's 100 percent normal. Don't let that deter
  you.

II. PRE-DATE

So you've got a date. Your mission? Before the date, figure
out what you're going to do together. (I know it would be so
much easier to figure it out afterward, since by then you'd
already know what you did, but unfortunately there's that
whole space–time continuum thing to contend with.)

When a man has to plan a date, he spends some time
sweating this very thing just like you do. Where, when,
what time? Here's how to get this thing moving in the right
direction.

Do

- *Google Him:* Why not? Hey, the information is out there. Nothing wrong with doing a little recon. I'd stop short of hacking into his FBI file, but then again, what am I saying? If I had that kind of access or skill, I'd be all over it.

- *Plan to Go Wherever/Whenever You're Comfortable:* Some people go nuts about the place/time of the date. Should we do a coffee date? A movie? Dinner? Is that too weird? Should we go out at dusk? Do people even say dusk anymore? What about the location—is a tractor pull too butch? Relax. Breathe. All that stuff that you're worrying about? It's all about the "meaning" of it, which, as you now know, will likely slip his attention entirely. Just pick something that you like where you can both determine whether or not you're having fun.

- *Have Some Ideas:* Ideally, your pre-date conversation won't be too much "I don't know. What do you want to do? I don't know. What do *you* want to do?" Doesn't matter which one of you did the asking; it's everybody's job to figure this out. Be nice. If all you do is go along with whatever *he* wants you to do, either he'll get annoyed that he always has to think of everything, or he'll, like, *love* it. And you'll be with *that* guy.

Don't

- *Worry about Your Shoes:* Sadly, he will never notice that you are even wearing them. Unless you've just wrapped your feet in duct tape or raw cod or something, in which case, not great. In fact, an excellent indicator that you wore the right shoes is that he didn't notice them. Unless you're out with a foot fetishist. Or a gay man. Otherwise, yeah, your shoe choice might not matter to him.

- *Plan a Hell Date to "Test" Him:* Don't plan to take him into some weird situation where you'll be comfortable and he will not, just to see if he can "handle it." That's called "being a jerk." Be nice.

III. ON THE DATE

Look at you! You're here! You're out! You're on a date! Now, let's give you some pointers on how to *not* screw it all up and force everyone to go home wearing a mask and cape to hide their shame. (On the other hand, if you both want to go home wearing a mask and cape to... I don't know, play *Phantom of the Opera?* Hey, your business, not mine.)

Do

- *Eat Whatever You Feel Like:* There was an article in the *New York Times* that revealed that women got more responses if they wrote that they liked steak in their online dating profile. The wrong conclusion? Steak makes men want to date you. No. Men don't give a crap what you order or eat on a date. Again, that's more "meaning" stuff. He's just not looking for it. Unless you're ordering the All-You-Can-Gorge, Conan-the-Barbarian plate of wings that comes with a bib and no silverware, you'll be fine. You know what doesn't look good? If you order a salad because some magazine told you to. That's just sad. Plus you'll be so hungry that you might not be able to...

- *Have a Good Time:* Seems like an obvious one, but remember that you're trying to determine whether the two of you had fun together. (I mean... that is what you're doing, right? You're not dating him so that you can have a bad time, are you?)

- *Remember That He's Nervous, Too:* Throw him a bone, okay? Listen, talk. You know how to do this.

Don't
- *Put Too Much Pressure on the Situation:* Ninety-nine percent of dates do not result in a lifelong commitment, okay? And that's exactly as it should be. Think of how few people you meet on a day-to-day basis with whom you'd gladly share a six-month road trip. Not too many, right? There is no shame if this date is not working out. And there's no upside in trying to force it to. You're just there to see what's what. And if you two don't have fun together, well, isn't that the kind of thing you want to know as early as possible?

- *Discuss How Many Children You Want to Have by Next Week:* Let him believe that you are there to meet someone and have fun (and are not just looking for a sperm donor). I know I said that men weren't afraid of commitment, but some of them might be afraid of being captured and used for their fluids alone. (It's not very badass if a woman wanted to date you because her clock was ticking and hey, you were nearby.)

- *Clam Up:* The first date is all about learning. Let him learn. You want him to know who you are so that if he happens to be the guy who loves that, he can find out about it.

IV. AT THE END OF THE DATE

Wow. Now I'm impressed. You've run the table. You've survived the entire experience. And now it's time to end the evening. How to do that is up to you. And when I say that, I mean that literally it is up to *you.* As in, it isn't up to him. Choose wisely.

First, a note on when it's okay to have sex.

I've gotten this question quite a bit on the website. How long must a woman wait to have sex with a man so that he doesn't think that she's a bad person?

The answer? Whenever you want. Seriously.

I'm sure that there was a time when a woman who put out was considered just this side of a hooker, and gentlemen wore hats, etc. But at this point, tell me if you can imagine this ever happening:

"Well, I wanted to sleep with her. But then she let me! Ugh!"

Lacks the ring of truth, doesn't it?

Not unlike the situation in which women worry about what to eat in front of a man, we're not going to be turned off if you do what you want to do. And if he is turned off by the fact that you had sex when you wanted to, uh, how is *that* a good guy to be with? (You *can* take this too far. For example, I'd have to recommend waiting to have sex at least until sometime after you've said hello. After that, though, it's all up to you.)

The most common mistake seems to be that a woman shouldn't have sex too soon or it will destroy the "chase" that men supposedly need. So you hold off and let him "chase" you, for fear of losing his interest. Please don't bother with this.

Here's the thing about "the chase." The guy who sticks around *only* because there's a chase involved is one who thinks of you as "prey"—yep, a player. Any of those times a guy bailed on you because the "chase" was over, that's because he was only ever in it for the chase to begin with.

So, some end-of-the-date dos and don'ts:

Do
- *Whatever You Want:* Again, if you want to kiss him, great. If you want to sleep with him, don't worry about it. If you want to do nothing, don't worry about it. Once again, men are not going to be delving too far into what the timing of the sex means. Not our bag. We're focusing on what sex does (i.e., "make our day").

- *Say You Had Fun If You Did:* If he had a good time, he's going to be trying to figure out if you did. Let

first date dos and don'ts, or you're not
wearing that, are you?

73

him in on the secret, ladies. I know the temptation is
to withhold that kind of information until you know
if he had a good time. But this thing's got to start
somewhere.

Don't
- *Assume He Knows:* The things that women have told
  me were "hints" (i.e., "leaning slightly toward him,
  hoping he'd kiss me" or, swear to God, "wearing
  tactile fabrics," which, since I'm not even sure what
  that is, I think we can rule it out as a "hint")... sigh.
  Look, if you want him to kiss you good night, don't
  send him that message by refusing to make eye contact, clamming up, and talking about insurance. No,
  I don't care if, in your little heart, you were thinking
  with all your might, "Kiss me, you fool."

- *Bank on Anything He Says About Calling:* We'll get
  into this in the next chapter.

- *Push to Make Plans for the Next Date:* Hey, maybe
  he didn't have as good a time as you did. Relax. All
  will be revealed. (Next chapter, next chapter.)

What if all I wanted from the date was sex?

If all you are looking for is to throw a guy down and do him,
boy, have I got some good news for you. In fact, you likely
didn't need to bother with the "date" at all. There's probably
a line forming outside your door right now.

Don't believe me? Read on for a cautionary tale...

The "Trick"

I knew a woman who once confessed that she had come up with a "trick" to get men to go to bed with her.

Okay. Let's say that again. A woman, okay? Spent time—time that she will never get back—devising a trick to bamboozle all the unsuspecting and uncooperative men out there into surrendering their delicate flower unto her.

Look, there are a lot of things that I don't know anything about. I admit that freely. But how can someone capable of a thought like this have a normally functioning brain?

My first guess was that her trick was to "be alive." And that one does work. It's a great trick. Men have not yet developed any counter to that one. In fact, that one works so well, it's almost not even fair that you ladies have it in your arsenal.

Oh, and for those of you out there who may be wondering what her "trick" is and how you might use it for your own benefit—please, you've got to stop. And you should probably not be operating heavy machinery either. Seriously, you need to put on a helmet and sit down in a pillow-filled room, or you are going to get someone killed.

And I hear you out there:

But Jeff, we want men to go to bed with us!

I know. I know that you do. And so let me clear up any misconceptions you might have about that. I don't know exactly what kind of resistance this woman imagined that she might be smashing up against, but—just in case she doesn't (or, God save us all, *you* don't) understand this—the male defense system against getting laid? Very flimsy. It really is.

And it only fully comes into its own in jail, at which point it can become very strong.

Yeah, yeah, yeah. What was her trick?

Look, do you want a trick to get a man into your bed? How about this?

Do...anything.

There's your trick. And if, for some reason, that doesn't work, do anything else. (You must have accidentally picked the *one* thing that wouldn't work.)

You want a situation where you need a trick? Try to get a man to get *out* of your bed when he isn't ready to leave. For that, sure, you might want to have a couple of tricks. (Personally, I think that most men will respond very quickly to talking of marriage and children, or ripping a giant fart upon his leg. Your mileage may vary.)

Okay, all right. If you really must know, here is what this woman used to do to trick the men into bed. If she was out at a club, she would go out onto the dance floor and dance really sexy... (gasp!)... with a girlfriend of hers (double gasp!!!)! Girl-on-girl action! And the men came running.

Yes, yes, fine. Look, I am not trying to tell you that this wouldn't work. Works fine. It is working on me right now. So why am I saying that this is a bad thing?

Well, mostly because it betrays such a drastic misunderstanding of the "male mind regarding sex" that it needs to be addressed.

Misconception #1: There is a male mind regarding sex.

You are attempting to weave a magic spell in order to control something that does not exist. You are attempting to hypnotize and bewilder your target man's mind in order to confuse it, so you can sneak in under his radar and get to the sexy parts. There is no mind; there is no radar.

This is not like one of those movies where the good guys walk into an enemy base that appears to be unguarded, and the hero looks around and says, "I don't like it. This is too easy. It's too quiet around here. It's a trap."

This is more like if a thief walked into some moron's unlocked apartment. With no front door. And a big sign that says, "My home will be left unattended for the next twelve hours. Please don't take anything."

The ease with which you will bed men is not a trap, ladies. Men don't appear easy. We *are* easy. If all you want is to have sex with a man, the only danger will be that *he* won't believe *you* are that easy, and he'll think, "No, no, it's no good. It's... too easy. Must be something wrong. It's a trap. Talk to me, Goose."

Misconception #2: This "trick" works, so it's a reasonable course of action.

Sure, it works, but how could she think that you have to go that far just to get a man in bed? Such a waste of time and effort. It would be as if you had something in your eye, and your "trick" for getting it out was to put a grenade in your eye. I'm sure that would work like a charm and get everything out of the eye. But maybe you can take a more subtle approach.

Then again, if you want to go through all of that, knock yourself out. We're happy to watch you skank it up with your girlfriends on the dance floor. I won't discourage you. Plus it will give all the guys who you do *not* go home with something to work with later on that night. (Remember how every man thinks about having sex with you? Yeah, this is where they get the ideas. And it probably will not be in ways that you would ever have authorized in real life.)

So since I am giving away the store here, let's talk about some actual "tricks" you can use to get a man to go to bed with you, shall we? I mean, let's say you are out at a club, and you want a guy to go home with you. What can you do?

Trick #1: Tell him that you want to have sex with him.

Works great. And you would be so surprised how grateful a man is when this happens. (Which is right on the verge of never, you know.) When a woman shows the courtesy to actually say to a man, "Hey, uh, I really want to have sex with you. Can we go do that?"—well, that's like Christmas morning.

Trick #2: Go back and read trick number one.

No, no, don't skip it. And when I say "tell him," I really do mean *tell*. Don't make it "clear" by your "behavior." You have no idea what you're talking about there. Not at all. You have no idea what is clear to us. Neither do we. But you know what is clear? Saying in words (or just going ahead and doing) what you want.

If you want to get a man into bed and are not sure how, you are going to have to understand this. Either he wants to be with you or he does not. If he does, no tricking is necessary. And if he does not… well, actually no, he probably does.

However, never assume we know what you are thinking. As we have repeatedly mentioned, we barely even know what we are thinking.

AAAAND… THAT'S ALL, FOLKS

That's it. That's a first date. Now you know what men are thinking during this whole insane process, and more importantly, you know how little we know of what *you're* thinking. Will this help you make getting, planning, having, and ending a first date any less stressful? Mmm… probably not. But then again, that's one of the reasons we like going on first dates in the first place. They're nerve-wracking; nobody knows what anybody is thinking; and who knows if anybody is going to get naked? Fun!

Next, we'll take a look at what to do now—after that first date is over and you're back at your house flipping out.

post-date debriefing and aftermath, or sitting at home freaking out

So you've had your first date with him and now you're home. Waiting. Wondering. Thinking. What's going to happen? Did he like me? Did I like him? Is he going to call? Do I want him to call? What's on TV right now? Oh cool, there's a special on the Illuminati and the Freemasons and conspiracy theories about…Okay, maybe that's just what I'm thinking.

What happens between the first date and whatever happens (or doesn't) next is one of the most confusing times for a woman. I think this has a lot to do with the fact that, since ancient times, the next step has always been the man's business. The woman's job has been to sit around and try not to chew her own arm off as she runs through a zillion possibilities of what the guy might be thinking.

Now, a lot of this has changed and continues to change. Women are more and more taking charge of the situation. But a lot of you out there still wait around and wonder what the hell is going on.

Okay, first step, take a deep breath and just relax. He will tell you EXACTLY how the date went for him very, very soon. Maybe not in so many words, but it's easy enough to read if you know what you're looking for.

Well, I come bearing good news. By the end of this chapter, you'll be armed with enough information to figure out exactly where he's at. And it's not nearly as complex as you think it is.

WILL HE CALL? OR HOW TO AVOID A TOTAL FREAKING MELTDOWN

Let's look at the possibilities.

At the end of the date, he says, "I'll give you a call."

Manslation: This does not mean anything.

When a man says, "Okay, that was fun—I'll give you a call sometime," what he's saying is that the date is over. That's all. It doesn't mean that he's not going to call you any more than it means that he will. It means nothing at all. He's just making noises at this point.

I know, I know. I realize this is frustrating for you. Fear not. This phrase doesn't tell you squat, but something else will.

But for how long, damn you?! How long?!

One of the things I hear from women when he tells her he'll call is, "Well, how long am I supposed to sit around waiting for him to call? If he would just *tell* me that he's not going to call, then I wouldn't have to sit around for two weeks waiting!"

Well, lucky you—you *never* have to sit around for two weeks waiting. Ever. You don't even have to wait one week. You have to wait a couple of days. That's it. If you went out on Saturday and the guy doesn't call/email/text by Monday or at the very latest Tuesday, that means he didn't have that great of a time with you. There are remarkably few exceptions to this time frame, such as that he was:

- Kidnapped by pirates and couldn't get to a phone

- Hit over the head with a frozen turkey that fell out of a zeppelin and doesn't remember who he is

- Buried alive in the family mausoleum and is still attempting to dig his way out

If he liked you, there are no great reasons why he would *not* have called within a couple days, max.

Does a text message count?

Great question, you words up there. What about text messaging—that slickest, quickest of communications methods that says, "Geez, I'd like to email, but I don't want to go all *formal-assed* up in here. Pff! Chillax, your *majesty.*" Does, for example, "c u soon," really convey a commitment to further dating? On its own? I'd say that's generally a big "no." I just don't think it's enough of a clue to go by. We need more here. And there isn't much less than a text.

A phone call, an email—these potentially involve punctuation, sentences, actual thoughts that require a brain; plus they take more than six seconds. (You there, stop laughing! I said "potentially," didn't I?)

I do have this nagging voice in my mind saying, "Hey, Grandpa! Maybe it's a generational thing, Mr. Walked-Uphill-Both-Ways-in-the-Snow."*

---

* Sometimes my thoughts speak to me in the guise of loudmouthed neighborhood kids. I'm seeing a specialist about it.

And who knows, maybe that's a fair point. Maybe for some folks, this counts as truly meaningful communication.

But here's what I wonder. Does a text message really show us enough to help us answer the second Big Question? Remember, what we're looking for here is effort on his part to get himself some more time with you. More *non-sex* time, I'm saying. I'm not saying that we absolutely need a vowel or two to answer that question, but it wouldn't hurt.

Hey, I know that texting can be a fun and immediate way to flirt or to let someone know you're thinking of them when you don't have time for more than that. I don't think texting is a bad sign, certainly. But on its own, it's just not enough of a good sign. And I'm not trying to tell you that a guy who texts after a date won't put in more effort later. But if texting is all he does, well, he could hardly put in less effort than that, could he?

At best, I'd call texting a "placeholder" while you're waiting for a real clue (i.e., a call, an email, a parchment carried by Pony Express, etc.)

"GREAT DATE BUT NO CALL," OR MMM...NOT SO MUCH

This is a very common Google search that brings women to manslations.com: What happens when it goes fantastically well...but then he doesn't call?

Now, I know this never happened to you, of course. Just like I most certainly never told a woman I'd call and then didn't. This sort of thing just never happens to good people, right? Ahem. But let's say it happened to your "friend." What do we make of this?

Okay, so we've got the classic male mixed signal, right? You went out; you had a great time; and then… nothing.

Now, if we apply the Golden Rule (if there's a conflict between what he *says* and *does,* ignore *says*), then we can just drop the "I'll give you a call," right? We only need to look at the behavior. What are we left with?

1. He went out with you.

2. He didn't call.

Seems like kind of a no-brainer when you boil it down to that, doesn't it? But in the interest of thoroughness, let's apply the Two Big Questions as well.

1. Might he think that this behavior (not calling you) will get him laid? Can't see how. Even the dumbest guy has to know that you aren't going to have sex with him if you aren't nearby. And ruling out telepathy (and let's go ahead and do that), the only way to get you nearby is to contact you. So the answer to this one is NO.

2. Might he think that this behavior will maximize his time with you? That's a big NO on that one as well.

So, from this situation, we know that he didn't have a great date and doesn't want to date you. No need for any other explanation. This is what we in the manslations business call an "open-and-shut case."

But then why, by Zeus's mighty thunderbolt, would he tell me he'd call?

Men have told you they were going to call to avoid telling you that they were not going to call, which would have been awkward. We don't like being the bad guy and would prefer not telling you we don't like you to your face. Or any other part of you.

It's all about reputation, in a way. If a woman tells a man, "Look, it's not going to happen, so don't call me, okay, chief?" it's not really even considered rude. It's almost expected. If, however, a man says, "Look, I'm not going to call you, okay?" he's a big jerk.

If a guy likes you, what possible reason could there be for him not to call? If he had so much fun with you, why would he deprive himself of even more fun?

More good news: You don't even WANT that guy to call you. If he isn't dying to call you, he's not the right guy. The right guy will always be very excited to call you. And soon.

That's so not true. I went out with a guy, and he called me three weeks later.

Right, but that was at one in the morning, and he wanted you to come over to his apartment for sex.

Uh... no it... er... ahem... was not.

Uh-huh. Sure, it was. Otherwise, why the wait?

Then why doesn't he leave out the "I'll call you" part and just say good night?

This one is harder to explain. And not because it involves big words I don't know. This is a sticky situation, because it involves something negative about women.

Women (he said while ducking) Want Men to Lie.

No! We want the truth! If a guy would just tell us right then and there, we could get on with our lives and not torture ourselves about why he didn't call.

Well, there's a problem right there. You think there is some mystery about why he didn't call. He didn't call because he doesn't want to talk to you. Is that the conversation you would like to have had with him at the end of the date—the date where you presumably had a good enough time that you wanted him to call you?

You: "This was fun. We should do it again sometime."

Him: "Mmm, nah. I don't really ever want to have to talk to you anymore."

Well, he wouldn't have to say it like that.

No?

No. He could say, "Look, I really like you, but I'm just not looking for a relationship right now."

Exactly. It's not that you don't want him to lie; you don't want the real reason. You just want him to lie *better*. ("I like you a lot, but I don't want a relationship right now, and that's why I'm not going to call you," or whichever lie you like.)

Of course he's looking for a relationship right now. Who doesn't want to meet the perfect person right now? Sociopaths, that's who. Everyone who isn't in a relationship is looking for one right now. Everyone. (Remember that "fear of commitment"—yeah, the one he doesn't have?) If he didn't call you, that's how you know that he wasn't looking for *you*. And again, that is fantastic news. Cross him off the list of potentially dateable guys, and put him down on the other (much longer) list.

But he just got out of another relationship. He—

Listen. No man in the history of the earth has ever *not* called you because he liked you. If he likes you so much, why not just call, which you obviously want him to do?

Wait… do not answer that question. Let me guess. Is it because he is afraid of how much he is feeling for you right now? You guys went out; you had wine; you laughed; and he felt something. He felt something he had not felt in a long, long time. And it scared him. And he ran. He ran and ran until his lonely little legs could take him no further, and then he collapsed in tears on his bed of rose petals and angst? Right?

Golly, and I thought you weren't after the truth…

But there was this one time—

No. No, there wasn't. There still isn't. No man has ever, *ever* felt so much for you that he didn't call you back.

No, hear me out.

Sigh. Uh-huh.

He had just gotten out of a relationship, and he emailed me and said he thought he was ready but then realized that he was not.

So… what now? You think he was really in love with you but was just too relationship-ally tired to make it work?

Well…

This was after you guys had sex, wasn't it?

Uh…

Got it. This is what we manslators call a "lie."

Okay, so if he didn't call it's because he doesn't like me. I get it. But we had sex. What changed?

Nothing. He never liked you.

Remember "Sex Brain"? (See page 54.) Yeah, that guy needs to conquer stuff, take down saber-toothed tigers, stop international terrorism, and take you to bed. (Though probably not in that order.) But the moment sex has occurred, that part of the brain leaves the man. Quickly. And the man is left with the Everything Else Brain—more specifically in this case, the "So do I want to stay here or get the hell out of here?" Brain. The cuddle or flight response is very, very strong.

If he has sex, then bails and never calls, he doesn't want to date you. Why would he run out and never call if he liked you?

But all men aren't like that. This guy had been hurt before.

Sure, he had. Who hasn't? We've all been hurt before. This is a prime example of a scenario in need of a manslation. A woman sees male behavior, and since men don't leave many clues, she is left to make up a whole world to explain it. Let's go through some of these explanations.*

Stuff You Really Need to Stop Believing, Like, Instantly

No man has ever, *ever* stopped going out with a woman as a result of

1. Feelings that were too strong and frightened him. Think about it. What you're saying is that you are so perfect for him that he couldn't handle it. Such a curse you have there! Gosh, if only you hadn't been so great for him, he might have been able to allow himself to be happy with you.

   Come *on*. What's the simplest solution? That he somehow sensed that you were the perfect woman for him, who touched him in deep, important places that he couldn't handle? Or that he met you; it didn't really happen for him; and he bailed? Don't waste your time thinking about this man. He's not the one.

---

* Absolutely zero of these female explanations for male behavior have ever happened. Ever.**
** Read that other note. Don't read anything else until you believe it.

2. Fear of getting close to someone that he really likes because he's been hurt before and he senses that this relationship could be so deep that it could really hurt him again. You give us too much credit—we can't think ahead that well.

   Stop it. Stop it right now. I just heard your thoughts, ladies. You were saying, "Well, this guy doesn't know what he's talking about. I knew this guy one time who…" No. It might happen on doctor shows on TV, but that's because those shows are written specifically for women.

   And no, the reason men don't watch doctor shows is not because it makes him have feelings that are too intense and he can't handle them. Just step away from the steaming pile of bullpoop.

3. Being intimidated by a challenging woman. This one is really ridiculous.

   No, no, no, that one happens. I was dating this guy, and always called him on his "crap," and he dumped me.

   Yeah, sounds like you weren't as much a "challenge" as a "jerk."

   Again, no man has ever refused to date a woman because she was perfect for him or just too challenging. If you end up only dating men who are intimidated by how "strong" you are… well, you might want to explore the possibility that it's because you're not very nice.

There really are no exceptions to the three bogus explanations above. The red flag for you is that the explanations are awfully flattering to one side of the breakup. As in, "I am perfect as I am, and if only he could handle how perfect I am, then he would be willing to date me." Again, you're half-right. You're fine, just as you are. He just didn't want what you have. Your job isn't figuring out how to get him to call. Your job is to go find the guy who wants to call.

Honestly, think of all the times in your life that you have rejected a man. In any of these situations, have you ever been in love with the guy but dumped him because you couldn't handle how much you felt for him? As in, you loved him *too* much? Or you were perfect together, but somehow you weren't up to the task of loving him because of your last relationship? Ever been intimidated by how challenging a man was?

Come on. Of course you haven't. So don't make your guy have that imaginary thought. It will only drive you nuts.

SHOULD YOU CALL HIM, AND FACE THE UNHOLY DANGERS OF... UH... WHAT, EXACTLY?

On my website, I get this question all the time. After a great date, she's wondering if she should initiate contact to tell him that she had a great time. She's afraid that she's going to scare him off. There's a lot of misinformation out there about this.

My suggestion? Call him; don't call him; do whatever you want. It can't hurt. Here's why.

If he likes you, he's going to like that you called him. If he doesn't like you, he's not going to like you any less.

I think the confusion on this one has come from a leap in judgment that some women make.

They see it like this:

1. He and I had a great date.

2. I called him.

3. He blew me off.

Mistaken Conclusion: The call made me look clingy and psycho, and I spooked him and scared him off.

This is not how it went. If you called him and he blew you off, it went like this:

1. You had a great date, and he did not.

2. He planned to blow you off.

3. You called him, and nothing changed.

True Conclusion: He wasn't interested to begin with, and your call had no discernible effect on his feelings about you. Up or down.

Come on. Do you really think that he was sitting there at his house saying to himself, "You know what? I had a great time with her. I wanted to ask her out again. But then she called me! Ugh! And as if that wasn't enough, she told me she had fun on that date that I had fun on! Double ugh."

And if you *are* dating a man who only liked you until you called him to tell him you liked *him,* well, do you really want to be dating such a man?

AN ABRIDGED LIST OF THE VARIOUS GUYS WHO ARE NOT WORTH FREAKING OUT ABOUT

There are a few types of men who seem (again *seem*) to be sending weird mixed signals. Here are a few you would do well to avoid if you can.

- *The Romantic:* This is the guy who is obsessed with obsession. He loves that beginning time, loves getting you all caught up in a whirlwind of romance, flowers, secret meetings, urgency. And then seemingly out of nowhere, poof. He's gone, and wha happa? This guy is an urgency addict, and when your relationship stopped resembling a four-alarm house fire, he lost interest. Forget this man. He never liked you, per se. He liked the intensity of your time together.

- *The Therapy Addict:* This guy wants to analyze his every emotion, thought, and impulse, and give you the play-by-play. His version of being a badass is that he is either the most damaged person you've ever met, or at least the most enlightened person *about* being damaged that you've ever met. This guy likes trouble because it gives him some more chances to learn firsthand terms he read in self-help books. Avoid.

- *The Scorekeeper:* This man is interested in getting you into bed, because he needs to know he's still got it. And getting women into bed is how he knows. With this guy, the meter is running. He thrives on figuring out exactly what you want to hear, and then he tells you that. You'll know him because he's the guy trying to minimize the time between "hello" and bed.

- *The Collector:* He can't let you off the hook. Even after you two are done, he'll call every so often to "check in" or just to "see how you're doing." He's attempting to keep a whole lot of women interested in him. He's not sure he exists unless some woman thinks he's the greatest. You'll know you've found this guy when you can't get anywhere near him, except every once in a while—on his terms.

- *The "Honest" Player:* This guy will tell you straight out, "I'm not interested in a real relationship. I'm just too immature for that. In relationships, I'm big trouble." He's banking on you arguing *for* being with him, even while he's arguing against it. And then when he screws you over—and you can take it to the bank* that he *will* screw you over—he comforts himself (and sometimes you) by saying, "Hey, I told her the whole time…" Trust me, if a guy tells you he's a lousy boyfriend, he's always right.

---

* Don't take it to the actual bank. The teller will almost surely call security.

OFFICER, YOU'VE GOT THE WRONG GUY!

Look, everybody knows that the vast majority of men are going to be "the wrong guy." There seem to be endless ways that this whole dating thing can end badly. You didn't need anyone to tell you that (and if you did, well, there's a whole shelf filled with books that will tell you all about it).

But now you know to pay attention to what he does (and chill out about what he says). Just think how quickly you'll be able to weed 'em out. You could get through your whole address book in, like, ten minutes!

What you need to understand about men is that the *right* man is not going to play all of these weird games with you. You're not going to have to go nuts trying to figure out why the right guy didn't call, and you're not going to have to worry about calling him. You're not going to have to walk on eggshells trying to keep from frightening him off.

You're not going to have to do any of this nonsense, because the right guy is the one who is crazy about you. The real you. All of you. The right guy is the guy who can't wait to call you, can't wait for you to call him, can't wait to spend lots of time with you.

Anybody who isn't that guy, well, the best thing you can do with him is have as much fun as you can, and then let him go. He's not worth agonizing over.

CHAPTER 6 ● men and their things, or
sometimes a remote is just
a remote

No, I'm not talking about those things. I am not about to sit here and tell you about men and their genitals. That's for another book.

But isn't the male obsession with stuff just that thing where men compensate for their penises with bigger cars, TVs, or whatever?

No. Common misunderstanding. There is a certain school of thought that says that everything is all about men's "things." But I do not belong to that school, so get your minds out of the gutter. Yes, men are obsessed with the size of their penises. And since they are also obsessed with the size of their TVs, smart people with lots of time on their hands (and puny TVs, I bet) make the connection that it's all about the penis. But maybe it's more simple than that.

Men just like to keep score, period. Men are in constant competition about everything. This is why men like sports. There are "winners" and "losers."

Believe me, men don't spend a lot of time thinking about penises. We are far more focused on winners and losers. And penises are just one of the many competitions we might win or lose. Technology, gear, tools, cars, and sports are others.

What is it about men and their stuff anyway? Why do they love it?

Because they understand it. Technology either works, or it doesn't. And we can tell when something's wrong. And if it doesn't work, we're pretty sure that we can get it to work.

Basically, we like electronics because they are not like you. You frighten us. When you get mad at us, we know something is wrong, but we can't for the life of us figure out how to fix the problem. We try; we get into worse trouble; and ultimately we give an unconditional surrender where we say, "Look, I don't even know what I did. But I'm sure that I'm really sorry about it. Can we get back to the part where I don't feel tense and terrified that I'm doing something wrong, please?"

There's a big lesson there, ladies. If you can tell us exactly what we have done wrong, it will be better for everyone. No, we will never be able to just tell. Stop hoping for that. I just don't see it happening anytime soon.

BACK TO CAVEMAN TIMES

Another reason that men love technology is that it *does* stuff. The first item of this type was probably the club. Whoever had the best one killed the most elk. Awesome. And what about fire? Oh, forget about it. Whichever cave dude had the first fire made all the other guys go nuts trying to figure out how to make a bigger, better one.

But why does it matter?

I don't know. Why do you have five pairs of black shoes that are exactly alike?

They are most certainly not exactly alike! See, these have a little strap, and this pair has—

Please kill me now.

See, that's just what I'm talking about—you love those... totally distinct and different and in-no-way-the-same... shoes. Men get excited about, you know, different details.

Okay, fair enough. But every one of those pairs of shoes—

Thanks. Thank you, that's great.

Let's go through some of the main areas in which men are mesmerized by technology and see if we can determine why, what it all means, and how you can use this information to better understand your man. Or men who aren't yours. Once you know this stuff, you are free to go around understanding men at your discretion.

You can break man and his gadget obsession down into four categories, the first three of which date back to the earliest men (our friends with the pointy sticks and the cars that they braked with their feet, you know). The categories are:

- *Tools:* The stuff with which a man can do stuff to stuff

- *The Kill Brought Home from the Hunt:* The stuff that a man uses to impress everybody else

- *Controlling the Environment:* The stuff a man uses to exert his dominion over the universe around him

- *Badass Make-Believe:* Ways that men can pretend to be the awesome, cool guy that he's pretty sure he's not

TOOLS

Dating back to the very first tools, men have been trying to get a leg up on the competition. We're obsessed with finding a better way of doing stuff. It would be very easy to conclude that this was some kind of a drive to succeed, to improve, to leave our mark. Sadly, it's probably more about laziness. As in, "Oh man, if I get that new lawn-mower that has the GPS unit built into it, I bet I could program it to mow the lawn without me!"

History Break

Take, for example, the Industrial Revolution. This was a time in which men suddenly realized that if they set up a factory that would do a whole bunch of stuff really, really fast, they could make more money than any of their friends. And this gave them giant, raging, industrial erections. If there is one thing that turns a man on almost as much as a willing woman, it is a way to crush their friends in defeat through the clever use of impressive gear. Oh, that one feels really good.

And the two go together, hand in glove. If a man is

getting regular, fantastic sex, it might just make him think, "Good Lord, I am a god. I can do *anything*. I bet I could consolidate all the steel companies into one giant corporation!"

On the other hand, it can go the other way as well. "I swear to God, if I don't get some action sometime very soon, I am going to deforest the entire state of Minnesota."

Now, this can refer to literal tools, as in that 111-piece screwdriver set that he wants, even if he has no intention of screwing in 111 things in his lifetime. Or that Dremel tool that… I don't know what it does. I'm not even sure what it is. But it has, like, seventy-five uses or something, and I kind of want one.

But a "tool" could really be anything that gives him a powerful advantage over the modern-day equivalent of saber-toothed tigers. For example, the computer.

The advent of computers as a part of our day-to-day lives has… okay, sorry. Suddenly this turned into an article in the *New Yorker*. The computer is the pointy stick that brings down the mastodon. It's the wheel. It's the thing that makes a guy feel like he's CAPABLE: "Check it out! I can print— WIRELESSLY—from anyplace in the house!" He now feels like the mighty god Thor, seated at the right hand of Odin in Valhalla.

The computer is a big area of misunderstanding between men and women (you can also see this with cars, home theaters, and model trains, probably). It's the idea of *the best*. If you spend enough time with guys who are into computers, you'll hear them fantasize about the unbelievable gear they'll have one day. You'll ask what seems to be a reasonable question, "Why do you need that? What does it do that your computer doesn't do?" This is where the answers will get a little fuzzy. It's not so much that he *needs* it. It's that he can't relax knowing that someone, somewhere out there, has a more awesome computer.

Another fairly common example of this is the GPS device. GPS in the car means never having to ask for directions. Why can't he ask for directions? I don't know—why do you need five pairs of nearly identical black shoes? It is what it is.

He can't just ask for the directions because—and this is important—he's not lost. Yet. He hasn't conceded defeat yet. To ask for directions is to admit that he is not as much of a badass as whichever gas station attendant he asks for help. (Jack Bauer doesn't stop to ask for advice on how to strangle someone, does he? Pff. Bet your ass he doesn't.) I know it's frustrating for you because, well, what do you care? You just want to get there, right?

So there's your solution. If your man simply will not ask for directions, buy him a cool GPS tracking system. He'll install it, and it will *tell* him where to turn. Yes, I know. This sounds an awful lot like asking for directions. But he'll still feel like he solved the problem himself—through superior technology.

As we'll discuss in the special Holiday chapter, tools make excellent gifts for a man. I know, I know. You don't want to get him something functional; you want to get him something special. Trust me—whatever he's into, if you can get him some kind of a gadget or tool that makes it easier, better, or cooler, to him *that's* special. And I promise he'll be very, very psyched.(You'll be able to tell when he brags to his idiot friends about how awesome his new doodad is.)

THE KILL BROUGHT HOME FROM THE HUNT

These items are the kind of thing that primitive men brought back to the cave to impress the women and to make the other men feel like inadequate cave jerks. In this situation, it's often a "bigger is better" mentality. You can expect your man to show you these things as if you might be impressed by them. If you are as smart as my woman is, you'll ooh and aah all over the place and tell him how impressed you are. Then he can go on about his business knowing that he's a man.

Now, this isn't to say that he always understands what might be impressive to you. You know how a cat will often bring you a dead mouse? Why would he do that? Is it because he wanted to disgust you? Not in the least. It's just that

1. He really likes mice,

2. He was very proud of the fact that he killed it, and

3. All he has to offer is a dead mouse.

This is like when your man tells you about something really cool that he did at the office with the new scanner/printer/fax machine. He's not trying to bore you to death. He just wants you to know that he did something cool and that he's a capable man who deserves you. If he had something better than that dead mouse of a boring story about how he saved the company seventy-nine dollars per decade on Post-it notes, believe me, he'd give it to you.

Here are a few examples:

The Car

Ah, the automobile. The radiator, the piston. The immortal carburetor. Er… okay, to my eternal shame, I don't know anything about cars. But as a guy, I feel that I should know. And even though I don't know the difference between a V8 and a bag of dirt, I'm intrigued by them. (Cars, not bags of dirt.)

Since cars were invented, men have wanted them. First, they want a car. Then they want a better, faster car. Possibly a Batmobile, if one is available. And when we were little, we were told there would be flying cars by now—men still feel a little betrayed that we don't have those yet. What is this fascination with cars?

- *Freedom:* When you're a kid, you're constantly waiting for someone to give you a ride. But if you have a car, you don't have to ask someone for permission to go from point A to point B. (Personally, I prefer to stay at point A, since that's where my bed is. But if you like point B, hey, having a car is the best way to get there without asking your mom to drive.)

- *Power:* Cars aren't just "as is." Some men know how to fix them up, make them faster, add in new stuff, take out crappy stuff. You can tinker with it, make it better than it was when you got it. When a man can

take this monster and make it even more monstrous,
Frankensteining into existence a vehicle that never
existed until he created it... pretty badass, no?

Again, I'm not talking about me. I can put gas in
there, maybe check the oil. But as a guy, I have to at
least pretend I *could* fix a car,* just not right now.

I was once with a group of men and women when
the van we were in broke down. There was no service
station nearby (and we needed to get back to solving
mysteries) so the men all drifted toward the front of
the van to see what was wrong.

The extent of my knowledge of automotive main-
tenance is that yes, in fact, that *is* where the engine
goes. Beyond that, I'm done. But my penis just drew
me to the front of the car, to peer into the enginey area
and see if... I don't know, maybe there was some
spaghetti coming out of some valve. You know,
something even I could diagnose. Why did I even
bother?

Which brings us to the last—and possibly most important—reason a man loves a car:

- *Chicks Dig the Car:* I don't know why. I don't even
  know if it's true. But guys are under the impression
  that women like fast, powerful, sexy cars. It's probably just my imagination. I'm sure I've never really
  seen some buxom bimbo sitting in the passenger

---

*Don't make a man feel like a jerk for not knowing how to fix a car. We can't know
everything. Some of us can't know much of anything. But... we're nice?

seat of a Porsche. One being driven by some bald-ing hamster of a midlife-crisis-o-naut.

The Peacock
Did you know that before this fellow got a job as NBC's representative, he was merely a bird? Wait, you did? Okay, so I'm a little behind. The main thing about the peacock is his tail. These guys have, as we all know, brilliantly colorful tails, which they use to entice all the peahens (hey, that's what they're called) to hump.

We look at this and think, "Those peahens are so stu-pid. Why would they think that a guy with better plumage is going to be a better mate? Pff!"

Well, I'll have you know that human males do this as well. We don't have brilliantly colorful tail feathers (well, *most* of us don't...), but we get as much as we can of the human world equivalent—cash. Or a brilliantly colored Porsche, say.

But of course, that stuff never works, right?

The Home Theater

This is the place in the home where your man has set up a rat's nest of cables connecting his TV to various speakers, DVD players, cable boxes, and surround-sound processors. This is an industry based entirely on a man's need to climb the next mountain.

High Def is one example of this phenomenon. High Def improves something that didn't really need to be improved all that much. Somebody figured out that they could tell a man, "Hey, there's a TV that's way better than yours. I mean, you can keep yours; it's fine. I'm sure it works… if that's all you want." My credit card is actually trembling at the thought that there exists a TV twice the size of mine.

Surround sound is another example of the home theater's potential glory. How many speakers does it take to make a man feel that his surround sound system is complete? *Answer:* as many as he can fit in his car. Hmm. Good point—he's probably going to need a bigger car, too. No, a truck! Something with four-wheel drive, surely! And so it goes.

If you have a man who is into his home theater and you want to make him feel fantastic, note aloud how much better his TV setup is than anything else you've seen on Earth. And when he tells you about the stuff he's *going* to get, become even more excited.

The ultimate home theater setup is the woolly mammoth of today.

CONTROLLING THE ENVIRONMENT

Ever since the first cave person realized that it was probably better to be a "cave person" than just a "person standing outside of a cave when it's raining," men have been obsessed with grabbing the world around him by the lapels and making it cry "uncle." Or at least we try. The most obvious example is the temperature in the house.

The Thermostat, or Fire for the Modern Man

This one we see in the typical northeastern dad. For those of you who do not know, this dad is obsessed with the thermostat. If you grew up in a warmer climate, I bet you have had the same conversation about your air-conditioning or something:

"Who's been playing with this thermostat? Huh? This thermostat is supposed to be set between 66 and 66.1333, and it's off by 7 microns. I'm not paying to turn this place into the Bahamas, here."

Now, at first glance, this seems to be a financial concern. If you move the thermostat, he will have to pay more. And in a way, that is true. But only on the surface. On the surface, yes, he is the one paying the bills. (Remember, this is archetypal. In my dad's case, not only did he not pay very many bills, I am quite sure he didn't know that he had a thermostat, let alone how it worked.)

But on a deeper level, this is about control. Dad is the king, the Lord Marshal, the chief of police, the secretary of defense. He is the bottom line. Or so he wishes. His life, of course, does not reflect this level of power back to him. He is a regular schmo just like every other guy in the world. He doesn't have much in the way of power or control or influence. Except, God help you all, over that thermostat. Oh, friends and neighbors, oh, you had better not mess with that thermostat.

I think it is also very important that you actually *can* mess with it. You can, and he doesn't want you to. It's very Adam and Eve, out there in the Garden of Eden, where God says, "You little jerks had better not even think of playing with that apple." And then you do, and he kicks you out of the house for the afternoon. Because you have learned the terrible lesson of the difference between Good and Evil (or, in the case of the thermostat, Mysterious and Boring).

The Remote Control

Another example is the man's control over the entertainment system in the house. As I mentioned earlier, much has been written about the remote being a surrogate penis for a man. Uh, you've got to stop talking that way. It just makes you sound foolish. Oh, unless it's 1973 where you are. Then you sound like a really innovative thinker.

Listen, the remote is *way* better than having an extra penis, okay? With my remote, I can control every device in the house—including the TV, cable box, surround-sound system, *and* Xbox 360—from wherever I am. I can even control my air conditioner. Top that, penis.

And besides, if the remote were, in your man's mind, an extension of his penis… uh… wouldn't he want *you* to be holding it?

So the main manslation for the Controlling the Environment section is this: If you can possibly stomach it, let him control the freaking universe. If you let him think he's keeping the planets and stars spinning to his tune by setting up the universal remote control, he'll feel like a man, and also feel like he deserves you. If you make fun of him, sure it will be hilarious, but then you have to live with a guy who feels like an ass all day long. Bad trade-off.

BADASS MAKE-BELIEVE

This area is a relatively new one, I think. Cavemen didn't need to pretend to be badasses. They were too busy wrestling with giant bears and hunting giant, deadly boars that were dead set on goring them. They *were* badasses.

Modern man? Not so much. Here are a few of the ways that men exorcise the demon of, "Hey, wasn't I supposed to be unbelievably awesome at something?"

Video Games

Why do some men obsess about video games? Maybe it's the same reason that women still play with dolls, okay? Oh, they don't? Hmm. Well, good for you guys. But a lot of men still seem to love, love, love playing games. Several big reasons here:

- They're fun, okay?

- They allow him to actually be a Navy SEAL for a second. Or a Jedi knight. Or a zombie-killing, undiluted badass of epic, universe-saving proportions.

- They are one of the ways that the computer industry gets him to buy new computers. ("This game is awesome… but you'll need a totally sick gaming rig to run it.")

- They are easier to figure out than you. There are rules, which, if men work hard, they can actually master. With you… not really.

So how might the best girlfriend in the history of the universe treat a man who plays video games? Funny you should ask. I know one of them. My woman got me an Xbox 360 for my birthday, okay? I'm not bragging. I only mention this because most of my guy friends gave me permission to marry her that day.

Now, of course, you don't have to go that far. You don't have to like video games. There's no reason for you to learn to play them or even listen to him talk about them if they don't interest you. (I mean, hey, if you want to let the solar system be overrun with the aliens of the Covenant, fine. *Be that way.*)

Actually, the coolest, nicest thing you can do about any of his "things" is to try to accept whatever he likes about them and just go with it. That's all we can really do for each other anyway, isn't it? You're never going to like all the same stuff. Sometimes the best you can do is let him feel fantastic about the stuff he likes, even if you think it's the most overblown, silly, ridiculous thing ever.

The main point is, don't make him feel like a jerk for liking them, because let me tell you, it could be a lot worse than him sitting around pretending to shoot stuff.

Hanging Out with His Idiot Friends

Ever since men and women have been getting together, men have been running off to hang out with their idiot friends. And women have been suspicious about it. What's the draw? Why do men do this? Well, in a sense, it's just more badass make-believe. When a guy is with his guy friends, he can pretend to be the total badass that he's pretty sure that *you're* pretty sure he isn't.

He can talk about guy things, and nobody asks him what he's thinking right now. It's not a knock to you, and it's definitely not a competition (you vs. the morons). Not for him, anyway. It's just an outlet for his testosterone. It's a reassurance to him that he hasn't become domesticated (even when, wow, he sure has). Plus, you know, these are his friends. He likes these idiots. What's wrong with that?

Try not to give him too much crap about this, as it shouldn't be any kind of a problem for your relationship. Well, not unless he spends two hours a night on the phone with the same idiot friend (as one woman wrote in to tell me). Yeah, in that situation, I'd start preparing yourself to overhear a conversation involving someone being unable to "quit" somebody else.

Idiot Friends through History
Look, this has been going on for a long time. For what it's worth, Socrates said his dying words to his pal Plato. His wife was sitting right there, and the last words go to one of his idiot friends? Yeah, I'm pretty sure there were a couple of awkward moments at the funeral when Plato and Socrates's wife were both standing there at the cold-cut plate.

The Crusades
During this time, there was a lot of, "Honey, come *on*. I have to go off and save the holy land, honey. No, no, I am not just looking for an excuse to go off and hang around with the guys. I am *not*. There are no women going along. Baby, it's a church thing, for Christ's sake. The archbishop is going, okay? I'm not going to mess around on you. Look, all of your friends are still going to be around. Why can't you just have fun with your friends, and I'll have fun with my friends? No, I'm not saying that I am *going* to have fun with my friends. It's… it's a figure of speech. It… oh man, I can't wait until the Dark Ages, when I can just put you in a dungeon or something. You are a real Ann Boleyn. No, that is not a threat. Look, don't make me choose my words, okay?"

Sports

I don't know how it got to be "manly" to watch, for example, a group of giant, muscular dudes in skintight, shiny, matching spandex pants throw each other around. But it happened. Why do men care about sports so much?

Have you ever seen a couple of mountain goats do that thing where they butt their heads together really hard? Well, this is classic male behavior. Men, like all male animals, like to beat the crap out of each other from time to time. Not necessarily to injure—just to compete. Whether it's with physical strength, money, brains, humor, or whatever is at hand, men seem to like competing for supremacy. And if a couple of guys are huge losers and they know they are huge losers, you guessed it. They'll compete for the honor of which one is the hugest loser.

Not much of a mystery here. In nature, whoever wins these things gets the best females and first crack at the best food. In human society, the men who win whatever weird competition they are in will often get the women who happen to care about that particular weird competition, plus all the best stuff involved. Could be money, could be cars, could be Star Wars figures.

So the next time you see two guys competing and you think it's juvenile, rest assured that it's even worse. It's not even human.

The point is, men love to watch sports because they get to see dudes run around and smash into each other. Just like we would be doing if we weren't so lazy, out of shape, and cowardly. When those guys run in for a touchdown, dunk right over the defender just for spite, smash a guy up against the boards, that's *us* up there.

We don't get to do that, because we'll go to jail and stuff. Plus, you know, I'm delicate and don't want to get my purty face mussed up. So I watch a guy who's getting paid to do it. He has fun; I have fun. It's a win-win.

What if you don't like sports? Hey, that's cool. But would it kill you to fake it? Kidding—we don't really expect or want you to. We just want to watch the game. So please don't do that trick you ladies sometimes do—the one where we have to have an important talk about the relationship during the game. You know, that thing where you want to make sure we love you enough to turn off the game and talk to you *right now*? Don't do that. We love you, we promise. But it's the eighth inning, okay?

The most important thing to remember about the badass make-believe stuff is that he does not necessarily expect you to share in his obsessions. Just don't make him feel like a jerk about them. Because, see, either it will work and you'll be in a relationship with a guy who feels like a jerk about stuff he likes, which… is fun, right? Or far more likely (and far worse), you'll be with a guy who learns that he has to hide stuff from you. That leads to all kinds of lousy places, and I assure you that one of them is not, "Say, video games really *are* something to be ashamed of! I think I'll learn French!"

SO WHERE DOES ALL THIS INFORMATION LEAVE YOU, THE COMMON WOMAN?

Well, I think we've established that the average man is obsessed with stuff as it relates to his value as a capable, strong, cool guy. If you want to make your man feel good about himself (and about *you*), you want to allow him to feel like he conquered the elements when he sets up the remote control to the ceiling fan, even if it's just as easy to pull the chain like you always used to. You want to make him feel victorious when he gets the new TV, and holy cow, High Def really does make a difference! When he wants a ratchet set for Christmas, don't get him a scarf, even if it will look really cute on him, unless you give it to him in addition to the ratchet set.

A little later, we'll talk about how to teach him to understand the kinds of stuff that you like (so you don't end up getting a ratchet set for Christmas, even if you really need one for some reason).

CHAPTER 7 ● having "the talk," or how to communicate with a man without causing him to exit via the fire escape

Ah, language, words, communication. The one achievement that has separated us from the rest of the animals* and allowed us to create our civilization. Then again, given that I have never seen one manatee say to another one, "So what the hell's *that* supposed to mean?!" and then storm off crying, maybe it's debatable how much of an "achievement" it really is.

So why do we need to talk in a relationship? Well, from time to time, something's not how it's supposed to be. Either something's not happening or something else is happening too often. I don't really know—I'm a man. When and why we have The Talk is usually your department, not mine.

Enter four words guaranteed to strike terror into the heart of the bravest of men: "We need to talk..." And unless you're dating a firefighter or something, you're not with the "bravest of men." You're just with some guy. So yeah, he's probably pretty nervous. Even just typing those four words, the hairs on the back of my neck are up, and I'm eyeing the exits in case I need to make a run for it.

---

* Well, unless you want to be picky and count all that barking or waggling antennae or tentacles or whatever those little critters are doing to converse. Which I certainly don't. Just try ordering a sandwich by wagging your tail, and let me know how it goes.

For men and women, having The Talk has always been at best stressful and at worst insurmountable. I myself have had one or two of The Talks leveled at me in my time, and even when I've come out the other side thankful that it all happened, it was the same kind of gratitude you have for when your doctor does something incredibly uncomfortable to fix something that might have killed you. You're grateful and all, but… I mean, did you have to stick that thing up my…? Was that really the only way?

And with that unsavory (yet eerily appropriate) image firmly in your mind, I'd like to explain to you how you can have The Talk with your man with as little nonsense as possible. Some of what you're going to learn here is about him, and some of it's going to be more about what you ladies tend to do in The Talk that virtually guarantees tears, yelling, etc. At the end of this section, I'll get into some of the specific Talks that women seem to want to have, and how best to handle them in ways that won't make your man drop a deuce in his pants.

But first, let's get some general principles out of the way. There are some things you should know about men before you even start Talking. Let's say… three of 'em.

THREE THINGS YOU NEED TO KNOW ABOUT MEN AND THE TALK

- You'll be initiating The Talk.

- He does not understand anything about The Talk.

• You'll need to disarm his initial reaction (which will be... wrong).

I'll go through these three in depth, and hopefully by the end of this chapter, you'll have a much better sense of what you're up against and how to work with it.

You'll Be Initiating The Talk

Sorry if I'm blowing anybody's mind right now, but as the woman, you're going to have to get used to the fact that in the vast majority of situations, you're going to be the one who wants to have The Talk. Doesn't matter how badly you both need to be having this talk, we're just not as likely to start.

Think about it—having The Talk about the state of your relationship is never, never portrayed as very manly, is it? Okay, maybe on TV doctor shows. Or a movie in which the guy is dying of a rare disease, and he falls in love with his nurse.* But I'm talking about portrayals that your man has, you know, seen.

Go back to Jack Bauer. Imagine what The Talk would be like if they showed it on *24*. Jack would be sitting there with whatever future hostage he happens to be dating. She'd say, "Jack, we need to talk."

"What? What is it?" he'd say urgently. (He can't help it. He says everything that way.)

---

* I tried to think of a specific film for that example, but my brain refuses to store such things in its long-term memory. That area of the brain is too filled with character names from *Lord of the Rings* and the relative merits of upscaling DVD players vs. true High Def. I asked a group of typical guys if they could think of any movies like that. They gave me a look that was what I like to think of as the adult equivalent of a "wedgie."

"I just think we need to clear the air about some things," she'd say.

This would be the point where he'd start shifting in his seat.

"What's wrong?" she'd ask.

"Nothing, why?" he'd say urgently, as he started drumming on his leg with his fork and knife.

"You just seem a little nervous is all."

"What? Ha ha. Nervous. Ha. No, no, go ahead. Let's... talk."

She'd start. "Well, ever since you got back from defusing that nuclear weapon—"

His phone rings. He practically leaps for joy as he grabs for it: "I'm sorry, honey. I have to take this. Yes, Mr. President. Hostages—how many? When? Suicide mission? No problem, I'm there in ten minutes." And out the door he runs, calling over his shoulder, "I'm sorry, I have to go. I promise we'll talk about all of this later."

In most portrayals of men that are aimed at male audiences, having The Talk is exactly the kind of thing that gets interrupted by something that involves *doing* something (i.e., stopping terrorists from bringing nukes into the country, zombies attacking—you know, something that he understands and/or is actually good at).

Now, just because there are no portrayals of a manly relationship-talker, does that mean that your man will never be able to do it? Not at all. I'm just warning you that he hasn't seen the movies you've seen, and so he doesn't have any models to go by.

And no, I'm not suggesting that you make him watch a whole lot of these movies. (You want him to be awake for this talk, right?) You're just going to have to accept the fact that The Talk is, as far as he is concerned, your domain.

I've had plenty women write in to me, frustrated by this fact: "Why is it such a big freaking deal for him to just *talk* to me about this stuff?!" And all I can say is I'm sorry about that. We're not wired like you. We have feelings, and we have words—and frankly, we're just not great at converting them from one to the other. Personally, I have the same problem with the metric system. Luckily, I never dated a woman from Europe. (Just think of all the centiliters of pain I avoided.)

Language is one of those areas in which men and women simply do not look at things in the same way, and it's not even just the words/feelings exchange rate. It's the reason for talking in the first place. When there are problems (in the relationship or anywhere else), we likely don't go about solving them in the same way.

Remember, I'm not saying he won't have The Talk, and I'm not saying that The Talk isn't necessary for him sometimes. I'm just letting you know that it's likely on you to get it started. Unfair? Maybe. What can I tell you? Next time there's a spider in the bathroom, you have my permission to make him go deal with it.*

The next thing you need to do is to understand what he does and doesn't know about having The Talk.

---

* Unless (a) you are my girlfriend, and (b) it's really big.

He Does Not Understand Anything about The Talk.

Seems pretty clear cut, that heading. And I do mean "any-thing." Before you even get to all the things he won't under-stand about what you're saying, you should know that he's not even going to understand why you want to start.

Men talk to convey information. Facts. That's the stuff we focus on. Have you ever had a man relay information he heard to you about, say, a friend of his proposing to his girlfriend? It was infuriating for you, right? It probably went like this:

"Reginald asked Brunhilda* to marry him last week," he said.

"Oh, how'd he do it?" you asked.

"Uh... I'm not sure. I think they were at a restaurant."

"Well, did he give her a ring?"

"Uh... I assume so. I don't know."

"Did he get down on one knee, or what did he say?"

"Er... I don't know."

Actually, we can stop there, because that last one is going to be his answer for any further questions you have. You'll walk away thinking, "For the love of all that is holy, didn't you ask *anything*?" And he'll walk away thinking, "What the hell? I told her what happened! They got engaged!"

In his mind, he got all the necessary information. They. Got. Engaged. That's the important data, right there. Isn't it?

What you're going to have to realize is that what's impor-tant for you to talk about, he might not even know exists.

---

* Hey, I don't know who you hang out with.

Doesn't mean it doesn't exist—even stuff *in* him (i.e., feelings about the relationship, etc.), but it might mean that he's never, never going to just talk about that stuff. Wouldn't occur to him. You're going to have to prompt for that stuff directly.

Here's an example. If you were to ask a man, "How do you feel like our relationship is going?" I'd bet you a thousand bucks he'd say, "Uh, fine. It's great."

Does that mean that he thinks the relationship is going "fine" or "great"? Who knows? He sure doesn't. But what he heard was, "Do you have any major problems to report?" and his answer was, "Nope. No major disturbances, ma'am."

Now, if you prompted him with something specific like, "I want to talk about how things have been going since you moved in. Seems like you've been really distant, and I just wanted to see what was going on," well... okay, he'll still freak a little, of course. But at least he'll know why. Which is nice.

And if you've ever gone clothes shopping with a man, you know what I'm talking about. Most men don't, say, stroll around a clothing store just to see what's in there. We can't do it. When we need to go to a clothing store (i.e., when all of our clothes look like someone was shipwrecked in them or the Incredible Hulk just transformed back into Bruce Banner or something), we go there with one primary goal—leaving. Quickly. We'd leave the store before we even got there if we could, but we need those spill-proof khakis (or whatever). We go there; we identify what we need; we grab it, pay for it, and get out.

How does this help you when you want to talk to your man? Well, it will help you to get your point across if you can

- Be Clear: Actually identify what you're talking about. I know some women are allergic to this, but if'n you don't tell him, see, he won't know.

- Be Direct: Get to the issue at hand right away. If you tiptoe around it, not only will he not know what you're talking about, but he'll start dreading how bad it's going to be since you're doing all that tiptoeing. He'll lock down into crisis management mode, also known as "holy crap, what's happening, am I in trouble" mode. Bad mode for talking.

To illustrate how to do these things, I'll use an example of what *not* to do. Here's one of the things that women ask their men that they should never, never, never ask him:

Where do you see this relationship going?

A woman wrote me, furious that she just asked that one little question—and all of a sudden her man pulled way back, and he couldn't even give her a straight answer. You know, as if *he* was the one having a hard time being direct.

Even as I type that question, I have no earthly idea what she's asking him. What are the possible "destinations" for a relationship to be going? As far as I can tell, there's only "getting married" or "one of us dumping the other one." Those are the two places that a relationship goes. (Or maybe "a loud argument," if we're talking about the next couple of minutes.)

So as far as he knows, that's what she asked him: "Are we getting married, or are we breaking up? *Now?*" And unless he's wildly excited about one of those two options happening in the next couple of minutes, he's pretty sure he's screwed.

This is just a bad question. It has no value in the real world. Why?

1. It's completely unclear. He probably knows on some level that you're not asking him, "Are we getting married or breaking up, and right now?!" but he has no idea what you are asking. All this does is send him running for cover as he tries to figure out what he can say to keep you off his back until he knows what's going on.

2. It's indirect. Clearly there's something you want to ask him. But you don't want to have to come right out and ask it. So you ask this "pretend" question— as if you're just casually wondering this. This is one of those situations where you would do far better if you came up with an actual question and asked it.

3. It's impersonal. It sounds like that question that interviewers ask: "What do you feel is your greatest weakness?" By that I mean that it feels like it's not for him specifically, but one that you saw in a movie one time and decided that you would throw it at him. At best, it feels like it's a part of some "relationship checklist" that you put all men through. At worst, it feels like a trap.

4. It's probably dishonest. You likely already know that this is not the real question. But for whatever reason, you're going to put your man through this unfair question, rather than ask whatever it is right away.

What's funny to me about this is that the women who ask this question can probably tell you about fifty clearer ways to ask it: "So what if I asked him where he thought the relationship was going? All I wanted to know was if he was happy with the way things were going, and if he thought it was time to become exclusive!"

Uh... so ask him that stuff. You know, instead of that dopey question that you read in a magazine one time. If you go "fishing" with one of these lousy, vague questions, well, you never know what's going to show up on the end of your line. It will not likely be the delicious sea bass of clear communication. You're probably going to get the muddy, old, abandoned boot of relationship tension.

Which brings us to the third thing that you need to know about having The Talk:

You'll Need to Disarm His Initial Reaction to The Talk, or "Don't Move, or the Relationship Gets It, See?!"

You might have noticed that I used the word "disarm" in the title of this section. (If you didn't, don't worry, you can just go back and notice it now. There.) That wasn't by accident. When you say, "We need to talk…" his first thought will be that you're now in a form of hostage standoff.

You know what I'm talking about—in a movie when two parties are standing face-to-face, each of them holding a hostage at gunpoint. There are snipers everywhere with their sights trained on everybody involved, and almost nobody is relaxed and/or watching the end of the game that's on right now.

I know it sounds like an extreme reaction, but that's a lot like what we're thinking. Men learn that they are going to have The Talk, and their thoughts immediately go to, "What is the quickest way I can end this situation without trouble?" What you are going to have to do is to teach him that The Talk isn't about ending it quickly. It's about resolving it so that everybody is closer to the truth than they were at the beginning of The Talk.

This is going to be challenging since as soon as The Talk begins, we're back to the "problem-solver" mode. As far as he knew, all was well; now there's this Talk, and it's his job to poke the problem to death to get back to that part where all is well again.

Now, I'm not really going to tell you how to help him avoid this hostage-situation feeling. Unfortunately, it's probably just going to happen a little. At least the first few times you have The Talk. What I'm going to teach you to do is how to disarm it, so you can actually get to The Talk itself.

To do that, we're going to go through what you would do in one of those hostage situations in the movies:

- *Do Not Ambush Him:* First thing is you don't want to give him any reason to think that this is a trap that you have set up for him to walk into. Don't invite him over for dinner and then tell him that you did so in order to talk about XYZ. If you do that, you're just going to reinforce in him that there's something really scary about to happen here, that you're holding a gun to the head of your relationship, and it's up to him to answer you correctly—or else it's all over.

Plus, you're now telling him that he can't trust you. You've obviously been thinking about this but not telling him until you set up this situation just so. Makes him nervous. Makes him wonder how big a deal this must be that you felt you needed to do all of this behind his back.

Much better to just bring this stuff up as it happens. And it doesn't have to be a formal "The Talk... shall now begin," either. Remember, it's you who wants to have this talk. So you might do well to acknowledge that right off the bat, even with a roll of the eyes. "Look, I know this is so stereotypical, the woman needs to have The Talk with the man. But, well, I do. So here we go." You're not apologizing for it. You're just admitting that this is your thing and that you don't expect him to be comfortable with the whole thing.

- *Let Him Know You've Called Off the Snipers:* This is the part of the movie where one party drops his gun, holds out his hands and says, "Whoa, whoa, everything's cool. We're all fine here. Nobody's pointing a gun at you, okay? Everybody, lower your weapons." How to do it? Let him know you're not going to hold what he says against him.

He's pretty sure that you're going to be hanging on his every word and that he will be held to it. The stereotype here is that when the man says the wrong thing, the woman holds it against him for the rest of their lives. And possibly beyond, if you're into the whole afterlife thing.

When you're asking him to talk about the relationship, he's never, never going to be able to do it if he feels like he's being recorded and graded on his first try. Remember, he's not good at translating his feelings into words, okay? He's going to struggle with it some. If you want him to do it anyway, well, you're going to have to cut him some slack. Let him know that you're not going to hold it against him if he fumbles around with it a little. Which brings us to the next one:

- *Actually Call Off the Snipers:* Yeah, see, it's not enough to just tell him that he's safe, and then as soon as he makes a false move, you blow his brains out. I guess that would work. But like in a hostage movie, it'll only work one time. After that, you can forget all about trust.

The more you can get it into your mind that his words aren't his feelings, the easier this will be. And the less

you hold against him here, the easier it will be for him
to talk the next time.

- *Don't BS Him:* As we said before, he needs you to be
  direct and clear. If you're not, he can't relax. Just like
  a dog. When is a dog most likely going to bite you?
  When he's not sure where you're at. If you are pretending to feel one way but in fact you feel another
  way, he can tell. And it makes him nervous.

This reminds me of another example from the website. A woman wrote to me about a man who had
vanished soon after the resolution of a pregnancy
scare they'd had as a result of a "wardrobe malfunc-
tion" in the act. Always a scary one, right? These
two had been dating for a very short time, and all of
a sudden they were facing a moment that had the
potential to alter literally every second of their lives,
forever.

She told me something along the lines of, "I was
good. I didn't freak out or anything." She told him,
very calmly, that he shouldn't worry about it, that
she would take care of it. Stuff was never the same
between them.

My manslation of his disappearance was that her
reaction made him feel like he couldn't trust her.
She was freaked out, but she made sure not to *act*
freaked out. And so what could he take away from
that but, "I'm not sure what's really going on with
her. All I know is that whatever happened, she was

pretending that this potentially universe-altering moment was No Biggie. Uh… I gotta go."

I know she thought she was making things better by being calm. But here's a situation in which going 100 percent ape-crap might have been more appropriate. Not because ape-crap is better than calm. Because honest is better than not. If he couldn't tell the difference, pretending to be calm might have been great. But we usually can tell.

A Few Words on Crying

You know. Ladies, you know. You know that this is your trump card. You know that this is the one thing that will get you out of any jam with a dude. So don't use it.

I am not saying that you shouldn't cry. During the course of The Talk, hey, it comes up. If that's how you're feeling, it's how you're feeling. Honest is always good here, as I've said. What I'm saying is that you shouldn't *use* crying. Not because it won't work. It probably will. But it will also guarantee that The Talk is over.

See, we see you crying over there, and we think, "We made her do that. We are a big, fat jerk. We need to do or say whatever it takes to get that to stop us from being said jerk." Remember, for us, crying means either (a) a lead safe just landed on our foot, or (b) Darth Vader just told us he's our father.

But if you use this to get him to do stuff, ah, he'll catch on. And when he does, he's going to ignore your emotions from that day forward. The Talk should be about bringing the two of you closer together, not one of you tricking the other one into doing stuff.

BIG TALK LIGHTNING ROUND

In this section, I'll take some of the trickier examples that I've heard about, point out the danger zones, and offer some suggestions for your best route through.

When to Reveal the "Bad Stuff"

A lot of women who have written to me have asked about this one. How soon is too soon to tell him all the terrible, horrible things about you (I'm assuming stuff like diseases, murder convictions, and dog-fighting rings by the way they're talking about it), and how is the best way to bring it up?

Well, I have good news and bad news. The good news is that, with the right guy, it sort of doesn't matter. However you can get yourself through this stuff, the right guy is the one who is going to react just fine regardless of the timing or words you use. A good relationship deals with what comes through and turns it into just more good relationship.

The bad news is that, of course, there are plenty of guys you'll feel you have to tell "just right." These are what I like to call the "wrong guys for you." Look, whatever horrible stuff you've done (and I'm just sure it's terrible), you already did it, right? It's a part of your life. So, ah, ain't nothing you can do about it anyway.

The real answer is "when you feel like you can bring yourself tell him about it." Might you be wrong about that timing? Sure, but only with the wrong guy. The right one will have to be able to hack it even at the "wrong" time, or else he wouldn't be much of a right guy, would he?

I've had my share of "bad stuff" revealed to me in my time, and almost invariably, my reaction was that it wasn't as bad as she thought it was. Even when it was pretty bad stuff, it certainly didn't change how I felt about her. Really. Even when I didn't like her that much, now that I think about it.

I know you're still going to worry about this. And that's fine. I mean, it's going to happen, so whatever. What's important for you to know is that likely he will not be nearly as freaked out as you are. Remember, we don't think in terms of "meaning" in the same way that you do. We think in terms of "function." So if you did something lousy years back, what he's not thinking is, "That means that she's a monster!" It's more like, "Huh. So... so I do nothing about that, right? This is just stuff that happened, yeah? Okay. Cool."

Saying "I Love You"

This is a tough one for everybody. Nobody's ever sure when to say it, and if you blow the timing, everybody's pretty sure they're in for some weapons-grade awkwardness.

Here's what you need to know about how a man hears "I love you." Obviously, it depends on how he feels about you. If he loves you back, his initial reaction is probably major, pants-pooping relief. "Whew! She loves me, too!" He'll probably say it back right then. Yea, everybody's happy.

But what happens if he doesn't love you back? Well, it's important to know that, just like with the crying, he's going to be launched into "problem-solver" mode.

The Problem: I've got a woman who just put herself way, way out on a limb by telling me she loves me, and I'm standing here, saying nothing.

The Solution: Panic. He might say anything here. If he senses that you desperately need him to tell you he loves you back, he might say it, even if he doesn't feel it. Uh... I've heard. I read that somewhere. About a very... bad man. Sigh. What do you want from me? It happens, okay?

The key with "I love you" is, I think, that it can never be unsaid. My personal policy is that the way to know when to say this for the first time is that you can't possibly hold it in for one second longer. And only because *you* want to say it—never just because you need *him* to say it. If you say "I love you" only to hear it back, oh, you might very well hear it back. But it will only be because he's trying to solve your problem for you. Not because he feels it.

Little Stuff He's Screwing Up

These are your "dirty socks on the floor," your "never does the dishes," your "do I really have to ask him eleven times to mow the lawn?" He was supposed to do something, usually chore-like, and he's not doing it, and how can you get him to do it?

First, you should know that many men will try to "get around" actually solving these problems. We all know the issue:

She hates it when I come home late. Let me see. How can I come in late more quietly?

or

Okay, she doesn't like when I hang out with these specific friends. So…when I do that anyway, how can I make sure she never finds out about it?

This is just the way we do. Sorry about that, everyone. However, there occasionally comes a time when we know that it is actually far *more* annoying to sneak around the problem than to just fix it once and for all.

And by that I mean that we intend to fix it in a way that is not at *all* once and for all, but that we hope will do for the time being. Ergo…

Hmm. I have got to fix that toilet that keeps running. Now, I know that I could fix it for good if I were to replace this part. And all I would have to do would be to go to the hardware store, find a replacement part, drain the tank…okay, hold on. What if I took this garbage-bag twist tie and some gum…

But then sometimes we actually have to fix the problem for real. It's so unfamiliar to some of us that we almost don't know where to start. But once we get in there… well, we're going to really make a mess.*

So how are you going to move past all of this nonsense as quickly as possible? I heard a great illustration of a good way to approach this. A couple we know had this conversation. She let him know he hadn't done whatever stupid little thing it was, and he said, "Uh-oh. Am I in trouble?" And she looked at him like he was nuts and said, "Who in the world would you be 'in trouble' with?"

---

* I'm sure this is exactly how the American Revolution started. We tried to patch it up, tried to fix it piece by piece. Ultimately, somebody thought, "You know what? Let's take the whole thing apart and just replace the whole country. Dude, it'll be *fun!*" I am quite sure that if you were to read every history book ever written, you would *never* see this story told from this perspective. And I think that is just sad.

He expected to be trapped in this mommy/little boy relationship that we see on TV all day long, in which the woman
scolds the man, and the man, chastened, goes off and does
his chores. The problem here is not that it won't work on one
level—you'll probably get those dishes done with scolding.
But when he hears you talk to him that way, then he starts to
behave that way, too.

Basically, if you treat him like he's a little boy you have to
scold to keep in line, well, why would you think he'd behave
otherwise? And if you treat him like a man, same thing.

The key with this stuff is to refuse to go with the scolding-
mommy dynamic. It's seductive, especially for actual moms
who are dealing with actual little kids. But that's the thing—if
you have kids who you are trying to keep in line, ah, he's not
one of them. So if he's behaving like one of them, *that's* the
problem:

"Come on. I'd expect this from the kids—they're twelve,
they don't shower, they're little morons. You're on *my* team,
right? I really need you to help me figure out how to keep this
place functional, without running out the door and going on
a tri-state killing spree, okay?"

That's not nagging. Nagging is when you misrepresent the
relationship as the Wicked Stepmom vs. Dennis the Menace.
This is saying, "Hey, we're both adults, we're a unit, we're
together. Help me out and meet me halfway on this, okay?"

And the very best way to approach this? Completely
coldly, before he's even screwed it up. Definitely before you're
furious. Have a sit-down to come up with all of the chores,
who does them, how often, etc. Make sure everybody agrees
to what they're supposed to do. Let him know that you're

not going to just forget about this, but you're really going to do it and stick to your half. Then, if he "forgets" (and, er, he might), you've got his own agreement to work with:

"Come on. We don't need to talk about this. We agreed that every other week it was your turn to clean out the walrus cage. Get out there. It looks like Gustavus was sick this week."

Warning: Do not exchange sexual favors for chores. Ever. Ever. Why? Not because it won't work. Don't do it because it *will* work. And then you're a hooker who gets paid in chores. Which, I mean, if that's your thing, knock yourself out.

Escalation, or Are We Exclusive/Moving In/ Getting Married?

These are The Talks that men seem to be least likely to initiate. I'm not 100 percent sure why. I just think that we don't always think in these terms. A lot of men have some idea that they are attempting to stave off "domestication" and escalating the relationship can seem to be at odds with that.

That's the advice here. Don't make it about adding new restrictions. In the example of becoming exclusive, you're not saying, "Listen, I want you to be unable to see other people." I mean, you don't want that because you have some weird desire to deny him other women. You want that because you want to be closer to him, and the way you get there is to be the only person in the other one's life.

This isn't spin. This is being clear. If you tell him that what you want is for him to see only you, he doesn't know why. For all he knows, it's because you're trying to "tame" him or "test" him, or "break" him like a wild horse. You know, as a hobby. (I know that no woman has ever done that, of course. It's just a silly, silly example that never happens…) But if he knows that you are crazy about him, and you want to get even closer? That's clear. There's no question about agendas. You're being straight, and there's no reason for him to go on the defensive.

The timing is up to you. There's no good or bad timing for these sorts of talks (though, again, I'd wait until after the post-game interviews are over if you want his full attention. And I'd do it after his team wins, just to be safe. Kidding, kidding. Kind of…).

A very important thing to know about men is that you are *not* going to screw this up by screwing it up. And by that I mean it's not how you word this that is going to get him to want to move in with you. It's not the timing of the conversation that is going to get him to marry you. Or not to. These things, they just aren't affected by you "finessing" them. He either wants to become exclusive or he doesn't. There will never be a moment when he says, "Well, I was ready to stop seeing other women and just be with her. But then she asked me to do that in the dopiest way, and… I don't know. Now, I'm rethinking the whole thing."

Relax. The good news and the bad news is that you just don't wield that kind of power here. Be clear and be direct and really say what's going on. The rest is up to him.

Breaking Up

I've gotten some questions about how men prefer to be dumped. No, I really have gotten that exact question. Uh, I've done some informal polling, and it turns out that, strangely, they prefer *not* to be dumped. I know. I was surprised as well.

But you know, there actually are better and worse ways to do this. For him and for you. During a hot air balloon ride? Not great. (No safe escape routes.) Via text message? Honestly? Better than the hot air balloon. At least it's quick.

See, whenever anybody wants to dump his or her person, there's usually a bit of a debate whether to use the full-on Dump or the Fade. The Fade, of course, is where you pretend to stop existing and hope he doesn't notice that you're gone. With relationships longer than, say, a month, this will be about as effective as when a three-year-old "hides" by covering his eyes.

Anything longer than a month and you're likely looking at a real, full-on, no-kidding-around Dump. How do you do it? Two words:

Clear. Direct.

Remember those words from somewhere? Yep, same as with all the other Talks, you need to be clear with him here. Even if that means seeming cruel. I say "seeming" cruel, because I'm not talking about being Clear and Direct about what's wrong with him. What's the point? You want out, right? You're not holding a class called "What You Should Do to Fix Yourself, Even Though I'm Dumping You Anyway 101" are you? Wait… don't answer that.

So if not about what's wrong with him, Clear and Direct about what? Clear and Direct about the fact that you are *ending the relationship.* You're not thinking about it. You're not considering it. You're not "pretty sure" you "might need some time" to "figure things out." Leave him no room to think that there is something that, had he done it, you'd be staying. Don't leave him with the impression that there is unfinished business, or he'll become an unfinished businessman. Possibly with a briefcase and everything. (Probably not, but I don't know who you're dating.)

But why?! This is what the dumpee always asks you, right? Boy, if he only knew what your answer might be, I bet he wouldn't ask it. The fact is, I think men ask this one because they are looking for the problem so they can solve it. *Do not give them a solvable problem here.*

The fact is, with any breakup, it's never a result of problems. It's always only one problem: You are not the right people for each other. If you were the right people, you'd work out whatever problems you have. If you're not? What difference do the problems or solutions make if you're not the right match?

That's the best, most definitive way to leave a man. Let him know that there's nothing that he could have done differently. It's just that you've decided (not that you're "thinking" or "sort of coming to the conclusion") that the two of you just don't fit together in the way you want to fit with someone.

In a weird way, there's no reason for a breakup to even get very personal when you're dumping a man. And there's no reason it can't be kind and even friendly. The real truth of any breakup is that no one is really "leaving" the relationship—the relationship just wasn't the right one to begin with. There's no reason to be cruel about the fact that the two of you weren't born to be a match forever and ever, is there? You're just stating the fact—*fact*—that you've come to the conclusion that you two aren't the match that you are looking for.

Now, this isn't to say he's going to agree with you that you're not a match. That's why breakups are sometimes lousy. Sorry about that. Just stick to your story. For his sake and yours. Stick to the fact that you two aren't the right people, and don't get suckered into "softening" it for him. Trust me, this is as easy as you can let him down.

ALL TALKED OUT

And that's how you have The Talk with a guy. If you can keep this stuff in mind, you can really help make The Talk become less and less of a big freaking ordeal, until, ultimately, you can probably stop capitalizing those words altogether. He won't feel the need to be on guard, and you'll be able to just talk.

CHAPTER 8 ● manslating literature, TV, and the movies, or why nobody in the real world ends up with mcdreamy

Now we're going to take a look at some of the famous situations that we've all seen in movies and on TV. And okay, we'll look at "literature" as well. When you look at the portrayals of men in popular entertainment, you can see a whole lot about how men think. And how we think we're supposed to think. And how *you* think we think, even though we probably don't think like that. (There's a reason they call this stuff "fiction.")

As an added bonus, I'd like to think that this investigation will, in some small way, justify all the TV that I watch.

LITERATURE (THESE ARE THE ONES WITH "PAGES")

The Iliad

This one is an easy one. A Greek guy and a Trojan guy both like the same woman, Helen, who happens to be the Greek guy's wife. Paris, a hot young guy from Troy, comes to visit Menelaus (the Greek guy). Paris then starts banging Menelaus's wife while he is a guest in their house. Paris and Helen run away together, and Menelaus is pissed off. Menelaus gets some friends to go over and get her back. It results in a crazy, huge war that kills all kinds of folks, including most everyone involved. So what's to manslate?

Warning: Do not go to Troy with Paris.

Look, I'm not trying to say that Menelaus is a great husband. The man is a Spartan. He's a prick, I'm sure of it. I know that there are a thousand reasons for leaving Menelaus. And I won't refute even one of them. But if you go to Troy, not only will you not get to stay with Paris (he will get bored with you so quickly, you can't possibly imagine it), but Menelaus will bring all the Greeks and kill the hell out of everybody there. It's a nightmare.

Listen, Paris is an idiot. This wasn't about love. Oh, he *thinks* it is. But see, most men love the thrill of getting the impossible gets. And if a guy who loves that also happens to be good-looking, wow, will he be a really great boyfriend. For about a week or so. Loving, attentive, just about as poetical and romantical a man you've ever met. He will promise you the heights of passion and seem to deliver them in a frenzy of secret meetings—late night, early morning, whatever. (See "The Romantic," page 92.)

How are you to know that you are with a Paris? Well, there are signs. Has he fallen "in love" with you so quickly that, even though you feel incredibly flattered, you're a little skeptical? Follow that impulse. Does it seem like he *needs* to get you into bed and is telling you the most wonderful things in the world toward that end?

Remember the Two Big Questions: Is his behavior designed to get you into bed? Yes, it is. Is it designed to spend more time with you? Well, it might seem so, in a way. After all, it seems like he wants to see you all the time, wants to take you away from your Spartan lord, is unsatisfied with however much time you can have together, wants you to leave this man for him *now now now*. That's all well and good, but that's just *now now now*. As in, it's just during this entirely fabricated emergency situation that he's created for you two. What is the plan once you've broken up with Menelaus? What will your life be like together?

He doesn't know the answer to those questions. That's a warning. I'm not saying that Paris was lying to Helen. Not as such. He was lying to himself. He's not saying, "I am so in love with this woman, I don't even care that taking her home will start a war that will destroy everything I have ever known. I just have to have her." This is not true at all. No, he's saying, "Hurry up and run around with me like an idiot, before we figure out what a dumb idea it really is!" There's a difference between being a "crazy, passionate romantic" and just a "guy who doesn't think about stuff before doing it."

The point is that Paris doesn't love Helen. Neither, for that matter, does Menelaus. Paris is in love with the sound of his own voice telling her how in love he is. Menelaus is in love with owning Helen. So when Paris cons Helen into leaving, Menelaus is so pissed off that he has to go and kick some ass. The whole thing could have been avoided had Helen just dumped Menelaus and then said to Paris, "Oh, for Christ's sake, grow up, will you?"

Romeo and Juliet

Possibly the most famous romance in the history of everything. God knows why—it's between two teenagers, and it ends up with them offing themselves. Good plan, guys.

The manslation of this story is that men will go through anything when they're horny. Romeo's most important characteristic is that he's young. Young enough that he's still just getting used to hormones. Why does he climb up that balcony, even though her family will kill him for it? Literally, I'm saying—this isn't where her dad's going to tell his dad, and he'll get grounded or something. I'm talking about literally being stabbed. And yet there he is, staring up at her, making up poetry on the spot, risking disembowelment.

Men who do this do it for one of two reasons. Either they are too young to be able to fight the hormones—under the age of twenty-one or so—or they think it will turn you on. Men know that women want to be romanced. And even though we don't totally get it, some men realize, "Hey, if I act like a total romantic moron, those panties will drop so fast it'll be terrifying!"

In this sense, it's the same story as Paris in *The Iliad*. He didn't think it through.

TV (THIS IS THE ONE WHERE FAMOUS PEOPLE ARE AT YOUR HOUSE. FUN!)

There have been many shows on TV. For example, there was *MASH*, to name but one. That was a show about how funny the Korean War really was. (My information is that they were, in some episodes, exaggerating that aspect of the war.)

There was also *Knight Rider*. And *Baywatch*. And *Baywatch Nights*. But we are not going to manslate those Hasselhoffers.

We don't need to. The Hoff needs no manslation. He could
stand a gentle nudge away from his singing career, but we'll
let that pass for now.

But let's take a look at some popular TV shows and films
throughout the ages and see if we can't analyze some of the
male characters and their behavior.

24 and Jack Bauer

Kiefer Sutherland plays Jack Bauer on the tee-vee, and this
will be the longest day of his life. Bong! Bing! Bong! Bing!

As I mentioned in Chapter 1, the Jack Bauer Principle
can help explain how your man might think of himself. But
there's more that *24* can teach us. See, lucky for us, for all
the expertise that Jack exhibits in torturing, assaulting, or
generally punching people, Jack Bauer's greatest challenges
are in relationships. He can stop nuclear terrorism, biological
warfare, international incidents, and just about anything else
that CTU might come across over the course of your average
twenty-four-hour period. But that doesn't seem to help much
in selecting the women that he chooses to surround himself
with.

Background: Jack is a tortured soul. Probably from all the
actual torturing that he has done in his life. The man is a
killer. Literally. He is the epitome of badass, at an expert
level, with a master's degree in Badass-ery. An MBA. (I never
knew what that stood for until now.) He has done some really
awful things. He has gotten himself hooked on heroin for an
undercover assignment. He has tortured and killed people.
He once ate a whole baby, just so he could understand what

baby cannibalism was like. (Okay, they never actually said that in those words, per se, but it's in there if you look closely.)

The bottom line is that this is a haunted man. He is dark, dark, dark. No sense of humor. No real facility for anything but punching and shooting. As a result, it doesn't matter what might be going on in his personal life; he will drop it the second something happens that threatens national security.

Now, Jack Bauer has surrounded himself with some real idiots for lady friends. I mean, I am sure they're nice. But they all have clearly had it up to here with Jack's penchant for leaving the house in the middle of the night at the behest of the president. (We went into this tendency a little in "Having 'The Talk'.") They simply do not understand why he can't just say, "No, Mr. President. I cannot come out to stop a biological weapons attack that will kill millions. Not at 6:30 p.m. on a Tuesday. No. No. I'm sorry, Mr. President, but it is meat loaf night, and we have a rule in the house that no one is allowed to miss meat loaf night. I understand, sir. Yes, sir, I am sure that it is important. See, the problem is that there's this meat loaf…"

Here's where we get to the manslation of this type of man: He is being very clear with you about who and what he is. For this man, the woman will always come second to his job, and there is zero reason to believe it will change. I don't care how much he tells you he's going to "work on it." Remember, that's just what he "says." What he does is, you know, stop biological agents from getting across the border instead.

These girlfriends, wives, and what-have-yous have all decided that they are in love with Jack Bauer, if only he will stop being Jack Bauer. This is always a big, big mistake. Because one of two things will happen:

1. You will fail to change Jack Bauer and end up married to a guy who will run out the door at a moment's notice to kill folks that the president doesn't like. That's one option, and believe me when I tell you that it's the most likely one.

2. You will somehow succeed in getting him to agree to stop being what he is. And then you've got a neutered cat on your hands. Now, if that's what you're in the market for, well, you are a soul-crushing, selfish, evil person. Why would you want that in the first place? To "break" him?

If you are dating a man who is so committed to his career that he will always choose it before you, you need to ask yourself something: Why do you want to be with him? If you are hoping that one day he will stop choosing the president and punching people in the face and instead choose you... well, why would that ever happen? Or maybe an even more specific question would be, when, exactly, will that happen? On what day do you think this change will take place? Next week? Next month? In five years? Do you have any reason to think he even *wants* to do that?

But that is what I want him to do!

Right, I know—but he gets a vote on that, doesn't he?

But what I want for him is even better than what he wants for himself.

Ah. Now we're in really big trouble. See, you may be right. He might even agree with you. But it doesn't matter in the least. He's still like that, even though you don't want him to be. The question you want to ask yourself is, if he never changed—if I took him at his words and actions as who he is right now—would I be okay with being with him?

If the answer is yes, then accept the situation. If not, the only thing that you can do is to tell him directly, "This is not okay. I accept that you like running around, sticking people with syringes full of your various truth serums and whatnot or shooting them in the face. But I need someone who is going to be around. If you want to do all of that stuff, I respect that, but I can't be with you."

At that point, it's up to him.

You never have to accept a guy who doesn't put you first. But you are never, *never* going to change a guy who doesn't want to put you first.

I can hear you out there thinking, "He doesn't understand me. I can change this guy." No, you really can't. You might think you can, and you might even think that you are changing him. He'll choose you first for a while. Great. But it's an optical illusion. That other shoe is going to drop soon. He will get restless and feel the need to go out and save the secretary of defense from kidnappers. It's who he is.

Grey's Anatomy

Okay, I'll begin by saying that I have never actually watched this show. However, my girlfriend watches this thing religiously, and she has occasionally felt the need to tell me all about the plot after she has watched it.

Here's what I've picked up from listening to her, in between daydreaming about dive-rolling into a room filled with ninjas.

There are no manslations to be had, because there are no male characters on the show. Not one. There are female characters, and there are male actors playing imaginary men, who have been genetically engineered so that women will watch them on TV.

If you do meet such a "perfect" man in the real world, it's because he has learned that this behavior is the express lane to your pants. It is no more real than the TV show (which... you do know is not real, right?).

This goes for a lot of the men on shows where women are the target audience. They make them into these weird combinations of total badasses and emotional little boys who need women to take care of them. Men who could finally be the man they have always known they could be, if only they could find the right woman (i.e., *you*).

Men hate all these TV doctor shows, because we know you love them and we know we aren't like that at all. These guys are, for women, the equivalent of the giant, watermelon-sized breast implants in guy movies. They are fantasies. Watch them, have fun, pine away—but just know that real men aren't like that. On the plus side, Dr. McDreamy is never going to take out your trash, no matter what. But we might.

Everybody Loves Raymond

The classic situation we see on TV time and time again these days: The husband is a slovenly, pathetic idiot; the wife is a sage genius, and he's lucky she tolerates him. In these stereotypical situations, he always wants sex, and she doles it out when she needs chores done.

The manslation here is what we discussed in "Having 'The Talk.'" This couple has really taken to heart the whole thing in which the woman is Mom, and the man is the dopey little scold-able boy, just aching to be grounded. Again, the problem here is not that your husband would refuse the sex. Because he sure won't. The danger is that he'll take it, and then sex is no longer about him being attracted to you. You will have taught him that sex means that he has to figure how much work he has to do around the house before he can get some action.

Not to mention, I mean, sex is fun for you, too, right? If it's only fun in the sense that it is a tolerable compensation for clean gutters, I'm pretty sure you're doing it wrong. Just saying.

The Bachelor

Ah, the king of reality programming. Here's the idea. We get a bajillion semi-trashy women and stick 'em in a house together with instructions that they are now to fall in love with the same guy. The women comply; they hate each other's guts; they cry a lot; and the man will attempt to sleep with as many of them as he can before being pressured into proposing to one of them on camera. Great, great television.

On one hand, I can't believe that this one ever got off the ground. On the other hand, any chance you get to hear a guy have to somehow get across the equivalent of, "You are the most special… seven women I have ever known," you pretty much have to point a camera at that stuff.

This is a situation in which you can really see the disconnect between a man's sexual brain and his relationship brain. This guy is in hog heaven, with metric tons of surgically enhanced women all ready to strangle each other for the opportunity to drop their drawers for him. He doesn't know what to do with himself. And then when he starts kicking some of them off the island (or whatever they do), they are so confused: "But I thought we had so much fun together." You did. But that doesn't mean that he wants you for his best friend. He might be looking for a soul mate, but that's got nothing to do with whether or not he is *also* looking for a lot of sex. And congratulations, you were it.

The manslation here is that this is a perfect example of the Two Big Questions being ignored. Clearly, it's not enough to know that he wants to be intimate with someone in that house. He wants to be intimate with *every* woman in that house. Hell, when he walks through that door, the freaking cleaning lady better watch her back. But that has absolutely nothing to do with the process of looking for a wife. And since this show doesn't really afford much in the way of "quality time" for the contestants, there's right on the verge of no way to answer that second question. Good for some hilarious television, not so good for helping women understand how men look for love.

Alias

This show concept is a stroke of genius. A female super badass. Her specialty? Put on a wig and a sexy outfit, give a terrorist a boner, and then do a spinning kick to his face when he isn't expecting it. She uses the age-old weapon in the female arsenal: If a guy wants to do you, he'll either give you the secret code to the vault or, at the very least, he won't be paying attention when you clock him one.

But here's why the show is such genius. Not only do female viewers finally get to see a totally badassed female character (instead of the damsel in distress that's in all the other action shows), but men get to see a woman who is emotionally wounded and needs to be taken care of—*and* a super hot woman. And it was all in the same woman—such economy!

Why do some men want a "wounded bird"? It's the Jack Bauer Principle and the Pointy-Stick-Problem-Solver Principle right there. Some men like to think that they are the rock, the guy she can count on, lean on.*

Plus, she occasionally slugged it out with other hot women. Don't know why men like that one, but they do. I think guys just think, "Well, hell, they're so passionate about punching each other in the face right now. How long before they just start making out?" Sure, the "real" answer is probably "a really long time," but don't tell us that during the show, okay?

---

* Please, please, don't become emotionally wounded just to attract such a man. That's just nuts. And besides, if you're even considering that as a "plan," well, I'm sure you're plenty emotionally wounded enough already. Lucky!

Happy Days

Most guys who watched this show felt like they related to Richie Cunningham at best. The main thing was that, just like all the guys on the show, we all knew we were not as cool as the Fonz, but we wished we were. The Fonz could snap his fingers, and women would just appear and want to go to Inspiration Point with him. He could hit a jukebox and make it play. He could fix cars. This guy could *do* stuff.

Guys want to feel that *capable*. Men love to feel like they can grab the world around them, strangle it, and make it cry "uncle." The Fonz was the ultimate "Controller of the Universe." Think about that the next time your man jerry-rigs some weird thing where the microwave can be run by the remote control. If you can react as if he had just snapped his finger and Bill Haley and the Comets came on the jukebox, it would really help. And remember, just like Richie Cunningham, your man doesn't want his woman to think of him as the second coolest guy around. Even if you both know he is.

MOVIES (WHERE YOU GO TO A BIG ROOM AND SEE FAMOUS PEOPLE, FORTY FEET TALL!)

Titanic

This is a love story between Rose and Jack, two youngsters on the *Titanic*. They fall in love and then hit an iceberg. Not them personally, you understand. I'm talking about the boat. Did you see the film? Okay, good, you're with me—you know where the iceberg fits in.

Couple of manslations here. In "Men and Their Things" (chapter 6), we talked about man's need to have the biggest toys. Well, here you go. The world's biggest ocean liner: "Unsinkable." Thanks, dude. No woman would have bothered to do that. She'd think, "Well, what if we made a slightly smaller ship and sailed it responsibly, and then everybody could just have a good time?" And some guy would go, "No, no, no. Don't you get it? Then someone else will just come along and make a bigger one!"

For another thing, if it were the real world, the more attractive Jack was, the less wonderful he would be while he and Rose were deciding who got the honor of drowning. Sorry, ladies. That's just how it is. Just like really beautiful women, really good-looking guys go through life knowing that they are supposed to get what they want.

The big manslation in this movie is to remember that this, like the TV doctor shows, was not written to be realistic to men. Jack at one point draws a nude sketch of Rose, right? And this is romantic? Yeah, see, the whole "draw a sketch" move has never, ever, ever been anything but a "remove panties" lever. And I'm sure it works like a charm. But it's not about the ultimate romance. It's about, "Hmm. Wonder if she'll fall for this one." I'm not saying that you shouldn't enjoy the movie for what it is. But if in real life a man ever wants to make a sketch of you, just be warned that foreplay has begun.

Fatal Attraction

This is the classic "breakup gone wrong from the male point of view" movie in which Michael Douglas has an affair with

Glenn Close, after which she boils his daughter's bunny. She does not appreciate being dumped. The reason why this movie succeeded is that it is one of the nightmares that every man faces when he meets someone. You get in there, and then you can't get out when it's over.

When a man gets all skittish with you, just know that this is what scares him. He is not afraid of how much you made him feel or worried that he might get hurt. He is afraid you aren't going to let him leave, and then you are going to sneak into his house and boil his pet rabbit.

You might see this skittishness after the two of you have sex for the first time. Maybe he won't call quickly enough, whatever it is. You know what I'm talking about. We went through it when we talked about how to break up. The ol' Fade. He's trying to pull a Jedi mind trick on you and act like the two of you really aren't all that close anyway, so you should just let him slip away. He's hoping that you'll catch on, and he won't have to actually dump you.

You need to understand just how little you need to know to manslate this behavior. If it seems like he is trying to slip out the back door, he probably is. This is because he feels trapped in a situation that he doesn't want to stay in. Simple, simple, simple.

Men don't fear commitment for its own sake. And they're not afraid of intimacy, as such. They're afraid of signing an exclusive contract with the wrong woman and wishing that they were still freelancing. That's the fear. And if he doesn't think you are that woman, you can't convince him. Not even if you boil his bunny. In truth, if he thinks you're the wrong woman, he is right. You are the wrong woman. And if he has decided you're the wrong woman for him, then he's clearly the wrong man for you.

Either way, please don't boil his bunny, metaphorically or otherwise. It's just not nice.

The Godfather

Look, say what you will about the Mafia, but these guys get stuff done, okay? They make sure that they are the biggest, baddest, toughest guys around. I'm not saying that most men actually want to whack a guy. But I'm also not going to tell you that when someone messes with us, we don't have a little dream about him waking up with a horse's head in his bed.

In between the whackings, strangulations, and horse decapitations, there's some material we can manslate for the good of all. One moment comes when Michael is with a bunch of the mob guys (the "idiot friends" if you will), and he's on the phone with Kay. She tells him she loves him, and he won't say it back. One of the guys gives him crap about it. "Michael, when you gonna tell that nice girl you love her, huh? *Oh, I love you so much, if I don't see you soon, I'm-a gonna die!*"

Being romantic, being lovey? These things are not "manly," and our moron pals are simply not going to let us get away with them. Your best bet is not to fight that one. Don't bother "testing" him by asking him to be super sweet to you in front of these guys. It doesn't mean that he thinks that his feelings for you should be a "secret" or anything like that. He's just trying to avoid being made fun of for the rest of his life is all.

Star Wars

Oh boy, do men love these films. See, they have both the Richie and Fonzie thing going. They have Luke, the common dork. He is just a whiny little idiot, but then someone comes along and says, "The universe needs to be saved! There's a hot princess involved. And you're so special that we need you!" As I've said, all men are pretty sure this will one day happen to them. And the guy gets to defeat—*and then save*—his dad? I mean, *come on*.

In addition to Luke, we've also got Han Solo in there. The Lone Wolf. The "scoundrel." The badass gunslinger with the heart of gold. And in love with the princess. Just like in *The Godfather,* we've got a troublesome "I love you" moment that we can easily manslate. You know the one. Han Solo is about to be frozen in carbonite, possibly to be killed in the process.

"I love you," says the princess, in what might be her last words to him ever.

"I know," he says.

First off, let me say this. Boy, oh boy, is that guy lucky that he gets frozen right after that. If they had had five more minutes, oh man, would there have been some yelling about that one.

But the manslation here is that we've got yet another example of how the "cool guy" doesn't get all mushy in front of his furry and/or robotic idiot friends. And he doesn't do it when he's got to be strong. Han Solo is facing possible death here, and he's trying to do it without showing Darth Vader any weakness in the process.

Anything Futuristic and Post-Apocalyptic

In any movie that has a guy running around in a world filled with nuclear-fallout-induced zombies, you might see men in the audience get a little faraway gleam of hope in their eyes. What is this about? We all like to think that even though, sure, we're dorks right now… if that ever happened, we'd be the guy who could handle it.

We'd be the guy who figures out how to fight off the zombies, how to find food, how to survive. In a very real sense, many men believe that the only reason we're not badasses is the fact that the world doesn't need saving. I mean, go to the job, pay the bills, pick up the milk at the store. But if all goes to hell tomorrow, we know we'll be ready. (Even when, wow, will we probably not be ready at all. We'll be badassed outdoorsmen for about ten minutes. Then we'll get something sticky on our hands, and it's all over.)

The manslation here is that this is exactly why he won't ask for directions, even when he's really lost. This is why he won't ask for help when his computer is in pieces on the floor, and he's inventing new curse words. He's not just being a pain in your ass, and it's not just stubbornness. He doesn't want to need help. He wants to be the guy who, when it all goes boom, is the one who figures out how to survive and/or destroy radioactive monsters.

Say Anything

John Cusack. Standing out in front of the house. Holding that radio over his head to get her back.

That son of a bitch. Blew everything for everyone else forever. Basically, he set the bar impossibly high for the rest of us. Guys the world over knew it the second we saw it. From that moment forward, we all knew we were absolutely screwed. We'd love to be that effective a woo-er, and we instantly knew for sure that we were not. Thanks a lot, John. Appreciate it. Jerk.

Men do get competitive about this sort of thing. I have a good friend who came up with an incredibly elaborate way to propose to his girlfriend. Made us all feel like jerks. And that's why he did it. Oh, sure, he loves her like crazy, and he wanted her to marry him and all. Of that I have no doubt. But what he really wanted to do was to be the ultimate romance badass. For that, we have John Cusack and that friggin' radio to thank.

QUICK REVIEW

We all like to watch or read stuff that supports whatever weird view we'd like to have of ourselves. Stuff that shows us what life could be, all evidence in reality notwithstanding. You know and I know that men really aren't thinking of themselves as an actual Jack Bauer. But that is one of the images that we see over and over again. And these images, however unrealistic, are part of how we are trying to form an opinion of who we are in the real world.

Most men like to watch or read about stuff being *done* and the people who are doing said stuff. It's not primarily about the emotional journey, although that can be important as well. What's important about a story or character for us is watching someone take his shot and try to make something happen.

And that isn't necessarily how men behave in the movies and TV shows that were designed to get *you* to watch them. If you want a man to behave in ways that they do in the shows *you* like, it's going to be a struggle, because (a) he might not have watched them, so he doesn't know what you want from him, and (b) they're not real in the first place. No more real than Jack Bauer.

The best way to use this information is to know what you're up against here. Just know what the images are that he's been watching since he was a kid. And know that they're not so similar to the stuff that they've been showing you.

CHAPTER 9 ● twelve months of holiday confusion, solved

with special bonus section: gift giving from the mind of a genius

Ho ho ho, and happy holidays to you all. I have no idea what holiday is the closest where you are. But even if you are not approaching a major holiday, God knows that I am, so here we are. Stressed out.

I would like to run through a quick survey of all of the major holidays and how they relate to our subject matter. More specifically, I would like to show you how manslating can really help put many of the major holidays into perspective. Let's just go through the year, starting with one of the most terrifying of all:

VALENTINE'S DAY

This is the holiday on which a couple celebrates their love for one another, right? Well, ideally, sure. But in actuality, this holiday is all about the exploitation of male fears perpetrated by the makers of red objects.

Red teddy bears, cards, mugs, all kinds of candy, teddy bears holding mugs filled with candy. Roses of all shapes, sizes, and prices. Candy roses. Candy roses in the teeth of teddy bears that fit into giant red mugs that say "Cup o' Luv!"

I used to have a hard time with this holiday. Why? Because this is a holiday in which men are guilt-tripped into opening their wallets to guys in suits who have decided to say, "What do you mean you don't like Valentine's Day? You must not be a very good boyfriend/husband/lover. Shut up and buy something red, will you?"

Sometimes I would like to go to the corporate headquarters of Hallmark or Russell Stover with a shotgun and a list of demands and go out in a *Dog Valentine's Day Afternoon* blaze of glory.

And the diamond commercials. Whew. When I see one of those diamond commercials around Valentine's Day... I can't believe this is true, but it works. I feel like I am failing as a man for not buying some weird S-shaped diamond pendant that they have concocted for my woman to pine after.

And that's such a shame, given that I am failing as a man for so many other, far more practical reasons.

Valentine's Day is also one of those checkpoint moments where we have to attempt to reduce the complex question of the overall status of our relationships to the level of a gift. Are we at the "homemade card and mix CD" level? Are we at roses? How many roses? Is twelve too many? Is one too few? Or is one classy and twelve just tacky?

Basically, we end up spending this one playing thoughtfulness defense.

(See also "Gift Giving from the Mind of a Genius" at the end of this chapter for more on how men operate on such a terrifying day.)

After Valentine's Day, there aren't too many holidays that require any manslation for a few months. I don't see too much gender-related confusion on Easter, for example. Unless... your man really, *really* likes to put on an Easter bonnet and skip around the yard naked, hiding Easter eggs in places that will get him arrested in the South.

But really, that's less in need of a "manslation" than maybe a "shot of thorazine."

FATHER'S DAY

Father's Day is a great example of how little men are impressed by "meaning" vs. actual function. It's interesting, in the sense that it differs so much from Mother's Day. On Mother's Day, there are flowers and brunches—or at least there had better be, lest there be big, big trouble.

On Father's Day, what does he get? Maybe an ugly tie or a "World's Greatest Dad" mug? Who knows? Do people even do anything for Father's Day anymore? Most dads probably don't even know when it is.

What does this tell you? Look at it this way: If your man forgets Mother's Day, there will be much sorrow, gnashing of teeth, rending of garments—it's a total poopstorm. What if you forgot Father's Day? Nothing. He might even be relieved that he's spared the ordeal of pretending that he loves that ridiculous tie. But even if you got him the most meaningful gift in the world, he might be just as happy if everybody just left him alone for a few friggin' minutes.

But honestly, is anyone here because of their massive, crippling Father's Day troubles? No? Let's move on.

FOURTH OF JULY

If there's anything manslatable about the Fourth of July, I suppose that it's one of two holidays on which the man is expected to do something in relation to the food (the other being the carving of the Thanksgiving turkey, which we'll get to in, you know, November).

Barbecuing. I'm not sure why this is a manly activity, but I think it has to do with the inclusion of an open flame and a chance for serious injury. Makes us feel a little wild and tough to be taming such an element as *fire*, even if it's just for the purpose of a few hot dogs.

It's also one of the holidays on which a man is legally allowed, nay, *required* to watch sports. If he doesn't get to drink beer, eat grilled animal carcasses, and watch a ballgame on the friggin' Fourth of July, we might as well be kicking George Washington and Thomas Jefferson right in the balls.

HALLOWEEN

This is an interesting holiday for men, because it is a day on which all women choose to dress like strippers, once they are past the age at which their parents can supervise their dressing habits.

Could be a slutty baseball player, could be a cat that wants to jump your bones, whatever—as long as it requires revealing clothing. The kind of outfit that would make Lindsay Lohan look in the mirror and say, "Mmm... too slutty?" We *love* this holiday.

Just understand, ladies, that when you leave your house dressed like a nymphomaniac nurse, your intentions are more powerful, and the effects more widespread, than you probably had planned. You might have thought that you were going out to a party to dance with your girlfriends, the nymphomaniac pirate girl and the nymphomaniac Girl Scout, then maybe meet some cute guys and make out with them. That was your plan. And it's a great one.

However.

See, the stripper outfit isn't a smart weapon. It is not tactical. As you now know, when inciting a male fantasy (and dressing like a stripper has no purpose other than to be a male fantasy, in case you didn't, you know, notice that), you don't get to pick who you hit. Your chosen outfit has a massive A-bomb area of effect that will cause all men within sight of you to lose focus on the real universe.

The second you leave your house dressed like someone who might just flop over and have sex with somebody, we are all picturing ourselves as that somebody. I haven't even met you, and I don't even know what your costume looks like, and I'm already picturing it. And remember I'm nice, and I love my girlfriend. Doesn't matter.

Think about it from this perspective. As I've said, we're all (*all*) thinking about you like that every day anyway. (*All.*) Just imagine what we'll be thinking about when you're dressed up like a vampirette with a crippling oral fixation.*

---

* I'm not suggesting that you shouldn't dress like that. In fact, I am begging you to dress like that. Just understand the situation you're initiating. If you wear it, they will come. It's the circle of life.

So when your boobs are hanging out there at the bar and you are beset by slack-jawed idiots staring at them and compulsively talking to you, just understand that this is just the way that it will always be on Halloween. And it doesn't matter how quickly or harshly you shut these guys down—the second they are home alone, your memory will be theirs for the humping.

YOU-CENTRIC HOLIDAYS

These are your birthday and your anniversary. Lots to learn from some manslation here. Quite a few holidays smack you right in the face with the "means vs. does" stuff, but these two are the biggest. Your birthday and your anniversary, in fact, are *only* meaningful. (They are obviously not "functional.")

And what's the most common joke made about men and their anniversary/wife's birthday? We forget these things. Why? Well, sometimes we get a little fuzzy on the "abstracts" of a relationship.

Even though I love my girlfriend 100 percent, I don't really "get" the whole anniversary thing. But I know that she does, so it's cool by me. Hey, it certainly wouldn't be the first time I participated in something that didn't totally make sense to me in order to make sure I didn't get into trouble. (Now that I write that sentence, I think that's a reasonably accurate description of my entire life.)

The manslation of these holidays comes down to this: Just because he doesn't totally "get" them says absolutely zero about how he feels about *you*. He doesn't necessarily connect those two things in the way that you do. Now, that doesn't mean he should get a free pass on ignoring these days. But

you might have to help him understand that they're important to *you* without making him feel like a jackass for not
making that same connection.

THANKSGIVING

The second holiday on which the man must handle the food
in some way. He must carve the turkey. He doesn't know
how to do it. He doesn't really even want to do it. But if a
woman does it, he suddenly doesn't have a penis. I have no
idea why this is, but just let him cut the bird, even if he is
terrible at it.

Thanksgiving is also one of the big "visiting the family"
holidays. This is always complex. For one thing, men have
an interesting relationship with the woman's family. Why?
Because in many cases he is shaking hands with the man
whose daughter he nails on a regular-enough basis that she
feels like bringing him home to meet the family.

If you watch carefully, there's an interesting moment,
however brief, while these two men are shaking hands, when
the father has a big, big smile on his face, but his eyes are
betraying an urge to cut this guy in half with a chainsaw. And
not in a magic trick cabinet kind of way, either, where everybody's okay afterward. And in the eyes of the boyfriend, you
can see a moment of, "Hello, sir. Sorry I'm totally banging
the holy hell out of your daughter pretty much any chance I
get." This is just good entertainment, if you get the chance to
observe it.

This brings us back to holiday-related sports, only this
time combined with visiting the family. If you can manage it,
let the man watch sports on Thanksgiving. Even if he's not

a big sports fan, after a few hours with your extended family, there seems to be nothing more appropriate than watching a bunch of guys smash into each other as violently as possible. I don't even like football,* but somehow it makes me feel a little better.

Like, "Hey, if anybody says one more thing about which highway he took to get here as opposed to some *other* highway that he is *not* going to take to get home, I'm going to tackle him, and spike a ball on his forehead."

CHRISTMAS

This is a scary one for men. It combines the thoughtfulness required of Valentine's Day, the meaningfulness of an anniversary or birthday, the family interaction of Thanksgiving. Throw in the terrors of gift giving, travel, weather, and possible responsibility for setting up all Christmas lights, and you're looking at a level-five holiday emergency. I haven't even created a "level" system, but this one jumps straight to a five. That's how serious it is. I never realized how much Christmas stressed me out until recently. I just thought it was a coincidence that every year around December 12 or so I would begin a stream of curses that lasts until, say, January 3.

Christmas is pretty much all about gift giving. Yeah, yeah, yeah—peace and love and good will toward—sure, fine, sure. But for a man in love, hoo boy, it's all about what presents to get. Now that we're here at the Bar Exam of Holidays, the

---

* Fine, fine, I said it. I don't like football. It's un-American, I realize. Deport me to Russia; make me wear a Hello Kitty costume; do what you have to do.

Doctoral Thesis of Thoughtfulness, it's as good a time as any to discuss the male brain as it relates to the giving of gifts.

SPECIAL BONUS SECTION: GIFT GIVING FROM THE MIND OF A GENIUS

The stress of giving a woman a gift shows up regularly throughout the holidays we've previously discussed: Christmas, Valentine's Day, birthdays, anniversaries, etc. It's everywhere. And there's no help in sight. We've got commercials telling us one thing; we're pretty sure you're dropping hints, but we're not positive; all our guy friends are as clueless as we are; and all our female friends ask questions to which we don't know the answers (i.e., "What's her size?" "What colors does she wear?" "What kinds of things does she like?" etc.).

If we get it wrong, we of course know it immediately. But even if we get it right, we know it's only a temporary reprieve; and soon enough it's present season again, and we're going to be back on the hunt.

I want to start off by explaining just what it is that gives us such trouble, and then we'll talk about several male "solutions" to this problem.

First, let's look at how men view the whole process of giving/receiving gifts so that you can understand the issue and maybe even help out.

What Is a Great Gift?

If you ask your man for his answer, it will likely be very different from the answer you would give if you were to ask yourself. And why bother? You're you—surely you must know already. In fact, I'd say not to bother asking yourself any questions at all and just focus on what *he's* thinking, since that's the part you don't know yet.

As we've discussed several times in this very book, a man is likely to view a gift in terms of what it *does*, and most women are likely to see a gift for what it *means*, right?

How does that help us here? First of all, the ideal gift to get him will *do* something cool. Most guys love gadgets, technology, and tools. Lots of women don't want to give these things, because they're "not personal" or they're "just useful." And you can certainly give him whatever you want. But know that he *loves* stuff that is "just useful."

For example, I once saw a man receive a "voltage meter" from his wife for Christmas. It's just what it sounds like—it checks voltage and tells you stuff about it. You know, for when you look at one of your wall sockets and think, "Wonder how much juice that sucker's putting out?" Now, I know that sounds like the least personal gift in the history of the universe. But I swear, the look on his face was like those women on the diamond commercials.

Once again, let's go back to imagining a dog and yet another way in which your man is like him. If you're going to give your dog a present (and for the love of all that is holy, why do that?), what's he going to prefer? A really beautiful collar with his name engraved on it and the date when you first picked him up from the pound? Or how about a steak?

So that's what gift receiving is like for a guy, and it makes it very difficult when he wants to buy something for you. Most of the things that you might want for a gift? Yeah, he doesn't even see a lot of that stuff. As a gender we don't care very much about clothes, jewelry, and things that smell nice. Well, some men do. And they are called "gay."

Seriously, if your man can pick out a really pretty dress for you, make sure that he had help with the purchase. Personally, I don't even know what a scarf, say, is for. Do people still wear them? Is it like a Boy Scout neckerchief kind of a deal? And don't get me started about earrings, or I'll break out in hives.

And of course there's the actual act of shopping. We don't shop in a "thoughtful" way, for the most part. We look at "browsing" as a failure and waste of time. My goal in a store? Get in, get what I came for, and leave before a salesperson thinks to ask if they can help me find something. If I'm just looking around, I'm not doing it right.

The Appropriate "Gift Level"

Depending upon how long you've been together, your man might worry that he's going to miscalculate the level of the gift as it relates to how deep into the relationship you two are in at that particular holiday.

If you have been dating for a month, what does he get you? How about six months? How about a year? We have no idea. All we know is, if our aim is too far off the mark in either direction, we're in for a really uncomfortable time.

Men often find themselves playing defense. As in, "Okay, I can get her earrings, I guess. That's safe. But they can't have diamonds in them, or else I'm in big trouble. But they also can't be plastic, or she'll never have sex with me again."

Complicating matters further, when you are in the very beginning of a relationship, we know that we could give you a ring from a crackerjack box, and you'll love us for how sweet and thoughtful that was. But we also know that there is a moment when we graduate from that time. We're not sure when it happens, but we know when it does, we've got to get you something for real.

A Word about Thoughtfulness

I think I have finally learned what a woman means when she says that she "just wants her man to put some thought into a gift." I still can't actually do it, mind you. But I can mimic it in such a way that we're both happy.

If you ask most women what they want for Christmas, for example, it seems that she wants her man to have spent some time and energy on whatever it is that he's going to do for her.

And (and this is where we lose you) what the gift actually *is* doesn't matter that much, as long as we really put some thought into it. Yeah, even as I write that, I have a hard time following along.

We do about as well with "It's the thought that counts" as we do with "It doesn't matter whether you win or lose, it's how you play the game." We don't want to just get an A for effort—we want to get you *the right thing*. In the game of getting you a gift you love, we want to *win*.

So should you drop hints or not? Well, yes. But just so you know, saying something like, "My friend was wearing these really cool earrings the other day," is not a hint that we will pick up on. Probably not even if your boyfriend really, really cares. As far as he knows, that is the beginning of a really uninteresting story. You're going to have to really harp on it, or he'll never even realize you've given him a clue.

Barring some really clear, helpful direction on your part, what happens next is that as the holiday in question approaches, he will panic, desperately trying to remember what it was that you said that time... something about what your friend had and... aw crap, I'm *screwed.*

One Man's Solution to Gift Panic

Listen, I thought I was smart when I began to keep a running list on my computer of possible gift ideas for my woman. Every single time I thought of anything that even might be a good gift idea, I put it into this list—so when it's the second week of December, I don't have to wet myself for the next week and a half, trying to figure something out. But when I heard the ingenious plan that follows, well, I was mightily impressed.

A friend of mine, who we'll call "Ace" (at his request, seriously), apparently has had a long history of buying disappointing presents for his wife. Ace will try to do what we all know we are supposed to do—i.e., pay attention to stuff that she says that she wants. Great, right?

Well, being a man, he can't always tell the difference between a "hint" and "casually mentioning something you maybe sort of want." As a result, he has ended up buying her, oh, I don't know, say, gardening tools for her birthday. (I'm wincing in sympathy, my man.)

Now, I have no doubt that she told him she might like those gardening tools when they were at Home Depot one day. No one is disputing that. But evidently a woman doesn't want to receive utilitarian things like tools, cooking utensils, etc., as a gift from the man to whom she shows her vagina. It just doesn't play.

Now, Ace can understand that this was a mistake, but only after the fact. So—and here is the genius part—he has decided to invent for himself a safety net holiday.

A couple days after her birthday, Christmas, Valentine's Day, or what have you, is an optional holiday called "St. Stanislaw's Day." This day is not celebrated every year, just when Ace screws up. And he can then give her all the things that he didn't realize that he should have given her until after he gave her whatever dumb thing it was that he got.

This is true genius. And if you think about it, supreme thoughtfulness. Not only does it acknowledge the fact that, look, I am going to screw this up. Like, *a lot*. But also, by the time St. Stanislaw's Day rolls around two days later, he knows that she will have given away all kinds of useful intel about how what he should have gotten her in the first place. She might be momentarily annoyed, but at least she will now be clear enough about what she wants to clue him in. She gets the kind of gift she wants, and he gets to win.

God help me, I love this plan. Talk about snatching victory from the jaws of defeat.

Better Gift Giving through the Almighty Power of Manslation

So where does all this leave us? How can you make sure that gift giving is as fun, loving, and free from nausea as it should be?

Before anything, you should acknowledge that it is very possible that you and he think differently in this area. If all you want is for him to put some thought into a present, you have to know that when you tell him that, what he hears is, "Okay, okay, she knows what she wants, but she's not going to tell me. She wants me to figure it out. Crap, crap, crap!"

You're going to have to tell him, "Seriously, I don't care if the gift is useful to me in any way other than that it tells me that you love me."

And here are a few quick tips to remember:

1. Buy him stuff that does stuff. He will love it. Whatever he's into—whether it's computer games, tools, golf—if it does something cool that he is currently unable to do, he will be so psyched about it. Does this mean that you shouldn't go find him something really meaningful, like a framed print of the place where the two of you first met? Not at all. But if you can get him a GPS device as well? You will be the greatest girlfriend of all time.

2. Drop real hints. Ones that he can actually understand.

Note: Sitting at your house, thinking super hard about that beautiful pendant that you saw when the two of you were window-shopping at that town by the shore? Not a hint.

"Hey! You! See that pendant? Boy, I bet that would sure make a really great Christmas present for some lucky lady…" (insert eyelash batting, winking, and nudging here). Now *that* is a hint.

3. Cut him some slack, okay? If he cares about you, he probably really is trying. But just like that cat bringing you the dead mouse as a gift, his idea of "perfect" might not make any sense at all. But hey, he was trying, right? Isn't that, in its own way, thoughtful and meaningful?

So that does it for this chapter. If you are really mad because you wanted to hear some super cool hints on how to treat your man on Arbor Day, well… don't throw a tree at him. How's that? Now that I think of it, that's great advice all year long.

Happy Holidays!

CHAPTER 10 ● manslations to the top thirteen male conundrums, or real-life problems crushed to dust by the power of manslation

APPLYING WHAT WE HAVE LEARNED UP TO NOW

This section is all about Applying What We Have Learned Up to Now. (That's why it's called that—I wasn't being cunning with the title.) I'll give you a few of the fairly common "confusing" situations that seem to frustrate many of the women who come to my website, www.manslations.com. Since you've come this far, you should be able to manslate most of them on your own. And if you can't, I'm-a tell you. Just think how much better you'll be than those other women who foolishly have been procrastinating on buying this book. Exciting!

I saw my man totally checking out another woman's boobs!

Do nothing. Let it go. Look, there's all kinds of nonsense out there about how if a man's eyes are wandering, it's because he's considering cheating. I'm here to tell you that if a man's eyes are wandering, it's because they are attached to his head. (And if they're not, he's got enough problems without you yelling at him about this.)

As you well know by now, *this means nothing.* It doesn't mean that he's going to cheat on you. It also doesn't mean that he's not going to cheat on you. If you think that he's doing this because he wants to have sex with that woman, you are right. In fact, the only reason that you didn't see him checking out every other woman on Earth was that you just happened not to be looking when he was doing it. But this doesn't mean he's in any way interested in physically acting on it.

If you don't want to have to see him do this, though, it's totally fair to say, "Listen, if you're going to check out the waitress's cleavage, please just don't let me notice it, okay? It bothers me to see it happen." But try to get used to the idea that all men will always do this forever—and not just the jerks. In and of itself, it doesn't mean a thing. Let it go.

There's this guy at work. He is constantly looking at me and "flirting" with me. I give him no encouragement, but he will not take the hint. How do I get him to understand that I am not interested?

Well, you've got a few choices. One, get a really great boyfriend and introduce the two of them at some point, and have your boyfriend chat with him for a little while. This usually freaks out the creepsters, because then they see how different they are from the guy you actually like.

If that's not possible (and hey, I know you can't always go out and just *do* that), you're going to have to tell the guy to stop. Sorry about that. See, we are very, very used to getting a cool-to-cold response from you ladies, even when you like us. We just don't know if you're playing a game or not.

Also, our "trying to get laid" brain is fantastic at denial. It is able to see past any obstacles to the goal, even if the obstacles include "she's not even nice to me." The only way that some men will stop going after you is if they lose interest (sounds like this one isn't happening) or if they understand directly that there is no way the sex will ever happen. Well, also if one of you dies.

I caught my boyfriend cheating on me, and when I called him on it, he started screaming at me like it was my fault!

Ah, yes. The old Anger Smokescreen. Ugh. Sorry about that. Most guys learn to do this maneuver fairly early in our dating lives. It goes like this: You catch him doing something wrong; you have all the evidence; and yet he flips out as if you're the one being outrageous. He's banking on you not being confident enough to defend your point in the face of furious anger. So what he'll do is this: He'll get twice as mad at you as you are at him. His hope is that you'll suddenly wonder if it isn't all your fault after all. Just like with the Fade, this is yet another male attempt at the Jedi mind trick.

We all know this trick, though most of us grow out of it at some point. Usually the guys who are heavy into this one date women with terrible enough self-esteem that it actually works—he can actually convince these ladies that it's all their issue and he's the victim. Oftentimes they will even apologize to *him*! For catching him cheating! Seriously, it happens.

Here's how you can tell that this is all crap. Let's say you caught him cheating. You know what you know. If anyone is going to be angry right now, it's you. So anytime you feel that a man's attempting to convince you that you have no business feeling how you do and you're just lucky that he's such a great guy to put up with you, feel free to say, "Wow. Thank you. I *feel* lucky. Thank you so much for cheating on me. And I'm sorry, you're right. I don't deserve you. Please, please let me make it up to you by returning the favor." And then go out and sleep with his best friend. Actually, don't pick his best friend—do you really want to get with a guy who's friends with that douche? Sleep with his worst enemy. That'll learn him.

Remember, the Anger Smokescreen only works if you have so little confidence in yourself that you actually believe him when he tells you that you're being unreasonable for hassling him about, for example, keeping his online dating profile active even after you move in together. (Yes, that one really happened.)

He's cheating. How do I get him to stop?

This is a rough question, and it comes up all the time. It's one of the most common Google searches that brings women to my website: "Can a man stop cheating?" The real answer? You can't "get" a guy to stop cheating. You also can't get him to start cheating. He makes these kinds of decisions himself. He's a big boy. (At least he'd better be, or you're going to jail, right?)

Seriously, though, here's what I can tell you about fidelity in men. It is possible for a man to make a mistake. One mistake. As in, singular. And women can make such mistakes as well. It happens all the time. Now, that doesn't mean that you have to forgive him or trust him again or anything of the kind. A betrayal is a betrayal, and if that's the end for you, that's totally reasonable. But if you truly believe that this man made a mistake that he would never repeat and you truly want to forgive him, *it is possible* for a guy to cheat once and then not again.

That said, if a guy is a cheat-ER, as in, for his lifestyle? Yeah, that's not going to stop anytime soon. I'm talking about a guy who chooses to do this over and over again. Why would we think he's going to stop? Could he stop cheating just like the guy who made the mistake? Theoretically, sure he could. But he's not going to. This guy is making a choice. It might even be a choice he doesn't like. He might hate the person he becomes when he's cheating. But for whatever reason, he's doing it.

The only thing that you can do to "get a man to stop cheating" is the same thing that you can do to "get someone to stop drinking." Tell him how you feel; tell him what is acceptable/unacceptable to you; and leave it up to him to decide whether or not he'll agree to your terms. It's 100 percent up to him, and it's not your job to jump through hoops to get him to do you the big honking favor of not boinking other women. In fact, I'd avoid jumping through hoops for any reason. Unless you're a poodle. Or a circus tiger. (If you're either of those, congratulations on learning to read!)

I've been seeing this guy for about two months, and he won't introduce me to his friends. What's this about?

Well, obviously he either doesn't want *you* to meet *them*, or he doesn't want *them* to meet *you*. In my personal case, my girlfriend and I spent almost no time with our friends at first because we were having too much fun to want to give up any of our together time. She and I were busy being incredibly happy, we had limited time together, and I didn't want to spend that time with my idiot friends. And again, I say that with love. But dude, priorities.

Now, if your dude is spending a lot of time with his friends, and he meets with you in secret, well, go back to our two questions. Does he think it's going to get him laid? Yep, because, hey, it is getting him laid. Does he think it's going to further integrate you into his life? Nope.

And before you ask the next question, don't bother. No, you can't convince him to want to integrate you further into his life. All you can do is reward behavior you like and refuse to accept behavior you don't like, and see what happens. Just like with a dog… if a dog could leave whenever he felt like it.

Remember, whatever your situation is now, it's potentially going to be like this forever. Ask yourself, would it be okay if you met in secret forever? If it's okay, then great! You're good. If not, tell him. See what he does. Remember, you are not going to blow it with this guy. If he doesn't want you in his life and you want to be in his life, it's already blown. This relationship is already never going to happen. There's never any convincing.

So I'm afraid you're going to have to resort to direct honesty. I know, I know. It's another radical concept. But it actually always, always works in the sense that, whatever happens, you at least know you're then working from the truth. And if you

want to work from the truth, well, this is exactly how you will
do it.

I want my boyfriend/husband to come shopping with
me so he can tell me if I look good in stuff, and
that way, I can buy things he likes. Why is that such
a problem?

Well, first of all, you assume that he pays attention to your
clothes, which he mostly doesn't. You could wear the same
pair of earrings, for example, for the rest of your relationship.
Literally. If you don't tell him, he might very well not know.
Yes, I know that your ex-boyfriend noticed all the time, but
he likes boys now, doesn't he? Right.

But why can't he just tell me what he likes and what
he doesn't like?

Why can't you tell him which flat-screen TV looks better?

Because that's just a TV.

Right. That's what we're talking about. Different things interest us.

Also, when you ask a man for his opinion on clothes, he
has no idea what you're really asking him.

But all I want is his opinion.

Well, no, not really. Not if his opinion is, "You look really
overweight in that."

Well, no, but I want to know what he likes.

Uh-huh. Just not what he doesn't like. See, we're screwed when we get this kind of question, and we know it. We never know if you really want to know the real answer, if you just want us to tell you it looks great, if you're feeling insecure that day and need us to say you look great, if you *really* want this item but you promised yourself you shouldn't spend any money this month but, oh man, you really want those shoes…

How are we supposed to know what's going on there? By default, we usually just assume you want us to tell you that you look great. But then you try on eleven things, and after a little while, it becomes clear that we're telling you it all looks great. And then you get mad because we're not being helpful.

This is a close cousin to the times when you ask us whether or not you look fat. We know that the answer is never, "Wow. Yes. Yes, you really do. I am so glad you said something first because I did *not* know what to do about it anymore. Thank you. Thank you for being a big enough person (ha ha) to allow me to be honest about it."

I actually make it a policy early in relationships that I will never respond to that question. And it's not nice to ask us to respond. If you want us to tell you that you look nice, grow a pair of balls and tell us, "Hey, you there, tell me I look nice. Tell me I'm beautiful."

I don't know what you think would happen if you did that, but I will tell you right now that if my girlfriend said things like that (and she does), I'd break my neck complying (and I do). Finally, one I can win!

My friend's boyfriend compliments her on what she's wearing all the time.

I'm sure he does. And that means that he knows how to play the game better than your boyfriend. I'll admit that. But what I won't admit is that your friend's boyfriend gives a crap about her clothes. It's just not one of our things, ladies. We don't get it. And we *know* that you get it. So we know that our opinion is so "amateur hour" that we have virtually zero chance of saying anything that makes any sense.

Don't hope that we will ever be able to tell the difference between two pairs of shoes that are both black. We can tell that you're not barefoot, but that's about it. We just can't see those little differences that you see. Or… we just can't imagine that they are what we are supposed to care about.

Just teach him the game. Say, "Look, when I tell you I got these shoes for only this much, just tell me how great I am and how beautiful the shoes are and how they make me look hot and that I'm a shoe genius, okay?" And in return, notice the difference when he hooks up the new High-Def TV, even if you can't see the point. It doesn't have to make any sense for it to work.

The reciprocal blanket appreciation for stuff neither of you fully understands will work great.

What happens if I really do just want to know if I look fat?

Come on. You never do. You only want to know that he still thinks you do not look fat. If that's what you want, tell him, "Hey. Tell me I'm not fat, okay? Thanks." You just have no idea how quickly he'll respond to that. And if you want an honest opinion about an outfit choice, do everyone a favor and ask one of your girlfriends.

I want my man to be more thoughtful (flowers, cards, little reminders that he loves me). What can I do?

Well, as you of course know by now, men don't understand such gifts from birth; we must learn. We don't want to receive them, and as a result, many men don't think to give them.

You have to educate him about the fact that giving you these types of "meaningful" gifts, while it wouldn't do a thing for him, makes you very happy. And he's going to have to get used to it.

Your job is to make him understand that you and he are different in this arena. More different than he thinks.

And how are you going to do it? By hinting, right? Wrong! By telling. Come on. You're a big girl. If you want someone to know something, you tell him. If you want someone to know something without telling him, move to outer space. I hear space aliens communicate via telepathy. I saw that on the Discovery Channel.

The good news, again, is that if you tell him what you want him to know, *he will then know it.* If he doesn't know what you want from him, he almost certainly won't give it to you. I know he's supposed to listen and pray and wonder and hear your dreams and touch a tuning fork to your knee to divine what you're thinking. I know. The problem is that he stinks at that. Throw him a bone here, and you'll get your cards, your flowers, your sweet nothings.

In my life, I have had to create a sort of "meaningfulness hourglass" concept. What I mean is, I keep track of when I do something meaningful for my girlfriend. Buy her flowers, take her out for a special dinner, get her a card or something. Stuff that I wouldn't want to receive as a gift myself (because it doesn't do anything) but that I know that she will (because it means something). When enough time has gone by, I do something else nice for her, and I flip the imaginary hourglass and start the timer again.

I do this because I want her to be happy. But I also know that I will never, never actually think of these things without consciously reminding myself to do them.

Now, if this makes me the world's most wonderful man, hey, so be it. It is my cross to bear.

So how are you going to drop hints so that your man knows you want this stuff? Hmm. Not easy. I only learned it in response to some serious crying. My girlfriend had just had a horrible week, and, man that I am, I didn't think to get her flowers or anything. And she kind of flipped out a little. Can't recommend that route—it wasn't fun for me, and it sure didn't look very fun for her either.

You know what you can do here? It's sort of trickery, but it will work. You have to find an example to show him. Could be on TV, could be an ex of yours or a friend's boyfriend. You need to find an example of this "moron who didn't know how to treat a woman." You know, this total fool didn't even know that women like to get little notes, cards, flowers from time to time for no reason! I mean, how does a guy not know *that*?

Very likely, he'll say, "Pff! Yeah! What a jerk!" but he'll be thinking, "Holy crap. I gotta not be that moron." It's not even all that underhanded—you're just telling him a little parable about what happens to jackasses who don't know how to be thoughtful. Who doesn't love a good parable, I ask you?

This guy dumped me a year ago, but he keeps contacting me every couple of months "just to see what's up." It's not like we're still friends, so what is this??!

The Resurfacing Dude is a guy who gets a little lonely and feels like talking to any woman who might still like him. He's *not* interested in you. He's not interested in a relationship. Probably not even in sex (though I'm sure he'd consider it, if offered). All this guy likely wants is to believe that someone out there still thinks he's a cool guy. He's afraid he doesn't exist at the moment, and he's checking in with you to find out for sure.

If you want to stop receiving such calls, blow him off mercilessly. Don't give him what he's after, i.e., affirmation. Don't let yourself get angry with him though. He might interpret that as you not being over him, and that will still give him what he's after. Don't take his call; forget to call him back; and if you actually do talk to him, sound vaguely uninterested and maybe a little confused as to why he's calling.

He's harmless, so there's no real need to smack him down too hard. But if it's annoying to you, that should do the trick. I know it's a little passive-aggressive, but it's also effective and relatively kind.

He's totally committed to me—we live together—but he says he's "anti-marriage." And I want to get married.

I've gotten this one a few times on the website. And also it sounds... cough... vaguely familiar to me, personally... for some reason. Ahem.

Okay, we've already talked about how a wedding ceremony might not mean the same thing to him as it does for you. It's just how it is. Now, that doesn't mean men don't want to *be* married. We just don't really care about the *getting* married part. Not as much as, say, *getting* a sixty-inch LCD television. Now that's awesomeness, okay?

All right, not helping. So here's what I'd say about how to get your guy on board with the wedding so you can get what you want, and he doesn't have to feel weird and uncomfortable the whole time.

Ask for it as a gift from him to you. Given that he wants to be married to you forever, just let the "him being psyched about the wedding ceremony itself" part slide. Let him know that you realize that the actual wedding ceremony is mostly about you. (Because, again, if every wedding I've ever attended is any guide, it will end up that way.)

Tell him, "Look, this day is really important to me. I'm getting a sense that the ceremony isn't a big thing for you, but it *really is* for me. How about you make this day a gift to me? I know it's not your thing—it's all girly with all the flowers and the dresses and everything—but this is something that I want, and I'm asking for your help in making that happen, as a gift to me."

What this does is twofold:

1. It puts it in terms that he understands. You want his help, and you are asking for something specific. That's not hard for him to do.

2. It takes the heat off the part he doesn't understand. He might be freaked out by wedding talk because he senses that you want him to be psyched about the invitations and the centerpieces and stuff. And most men just are not and never will be. And as long as he loves you and intends to do so for the rest of your lives, is it really important that he also loves this ceremony itself, which is only going to last one day?

If you can be okay with that, he'll be way more on board and thrilled to be let off the hook. This should smooth the way for both of you to get right on the verge of all of what you want. You'll get the wedding, and he'll get an elk that's just begging to be poked with a pointy stick. He will be able to feel like he's being all help-ish and doing something that he can actually do.

You could also promise him a sixty-inch LCD TV. I don't believe in bribery in relationships, but… I mean, I'm sure he'd take it.

I was with this guy and it was going perfect. He was so sweet and thoughtful and crazy romantic, and then poof, he was gone. Nothing went wrong that I could see. Wha happa??

Ah, the man who goes poof. You found yourself a Romantic there, didn't you? Remember him? The man who loves the rush of falling in love. And more importantly, he loves the rush of *you* falling in love with *him*. But once things started to settle in, once you started to get used to him being around, his work was done. He was in it for the rush, not for you specifically.

The sad part is that many of these men are as baffled by it as you are. They don't want to be like this. And one day they might figure it all out and change. But not today. Let this one go. It's not that you had him for a while, and then he was gone. He was never really there to begin with. The clock was running down from the moment you met. The best thing you can do with a Romantic (or with anything, really) is enjoy the ride while it lasts and don't go too nuts about it later.

I'm with a guy, but he won't be exclusive with me or call me his girlfriend. How can I get him to realize that we're already in a relationship?

I've gotten several versions of this one on the website. The non-boyfriend. He's around on his terms, but he's not fully admitting you're together. How can you get him to just be with you? You can't. And what's more, you don't want to be with some idiot you have to "convince" to stick around. You want to be with someone who wants that all by himself, desperately.

How about this—do you want to be with a guy who didn't want to be with you until you somehow talked him into it? No, of course you don't. Who needs that crapola?

As my lady fair once pointed out to me, some women seem to feel that their relationship with a man exists objectively, outside of them. As in, if a woman is in love with a man, she thinks that she is responding to some capital L "Love" that is *out there*, and he must be feeling it, too. This leads some of them to have a thought very similar to "how come he doesn't know we're in love?" If he doesn't know it, it's because "we" are not in love. You are, and he's not. Nothing either of you can do about that. And again, who would want to?

He just will not pick up after himself, and it's gross. What do I do?

Many men seem to have a hard time keeping their things neat and tidy. Why is this? Well, the main reason is that the following things have never happened in the history of the world:

- A supermodel saying, "Wow. Look at how clean that guy keeps his apartment. God, he is so hot..."

- A Navy SEAL saying, "We're in big trouble. Quick, find me a guy who never—repeat never—leaves his socks lying around on the floor!"

Now, as you well know, if you try to make a man feel like a little boy as punishment for not cleaning up, he'll fight you on it. Why? Because the best-case scenario would be to do the thing right and have you think of him as a good little boy. Not awesome. My solution? Similar to the thoughtfulness parable. Give him an example of some other moron doing it wrong. Make him understand that the kind of man you like is a *man* who knows how to take care of himself. Not some little *boy* who can't pick up after himself. So unmanly, so unsexy. Like some lost little toddler.

See what I did there? Again, don't tell him that you think of *him* that way. Somehow let it slip that you know some *other* guy who is like that, and that's what you think of that idiot. This way, he'll think, "Ah, I don't want to be like that moron. I want her to think of me as a *man*."

Stupid and silly? Sure. But you want him to pick up those socks off the floor, don't you?

CLASS DISMISSED

I'll tell you what. If you don't know everything that there is to know about men right now, well, I have only myself to blame.

CHAPTER 11 ● final thoughts, or is that all there is?

(hint: yes)

Not my final thoughts ever, you understand. At least I hope not. But we've definitely hit the last chapter in this book—let's all agree on that, shall we? And yet I feel that I've barely even begun to scratch the surface of how to create a better world, a world in which men and women understand one another with absolute clarity and love. A world in which someone will pay me *gigantic* sums of money. I mean, I'm talking the kind of bucks where you can fly first class anywhere you go, and you never have to get onto a bus ever again.

Ah, well. It was just a dream, after all. Let's wrap this thing up so we can all get on with our lives as smarter, wiser, dare I say sexier people. What can you, the common man-misunderstander, take away from this book so that you can become a fully credentialed manslator in your own right?

YOU ARE MORE DIFFERENT THAN YOU THINK YOU ARE

Many of the really good arguments that happen between a man and a woman (and I'm talking about the truly spectacular ones that you can hear clearly from down the street) can be traced to a failure to understand just how different from one another the two of you truly are. It's not always so obvious to see this, since you're (presumably) both speaking the same language, using the same words and everything. But lurking behind those familiar-sounding words is a brain that might be absolutely nothing like yours.

We've spent most of this book learning how you can understand what's going on with him. (At least that's what I've been doing. For all I know, you've spent our time together trying to say the entire alphabet on one burp.) Here are some tips for how you can help him understand what's going on with you. Which, let me tell you, is much more difficult.

Be Clear

Throw him a bone here, okay?

I know that many women hate having to tell a man what is going on with them. And hey, you're obviously free to be as vague with him as you like. All I can tell you is that if you don't actually tell him what you are thinking, he's never going to be able to figure it out. And if you do tell him, he'll know. See how that works?

When you are mad at him and then won't tell him why, for example, he'll just never get it. Not even if you're really snippy for hours, I promise. Remember our doggie we've talked about: When you yell at that little guy, he has no earthly idea why you are so mad at him. He just knows that he is a bad doggie. And since he is clueless as to what set you off, he's more than likely going to be a bad doggie again sometime real soon.

You're going to have to come to terms with the fact that you are not always very clear with us, even when you think you are.

I can hear some of you out there saying, "Well, you men aren't clear either!"

Yes. Yes we are. But you are so complex that you think we must be, too. We really aren't. We're pretty simple for the most part. But you women—you have different sets of rules for different types of situations and try as we might, we just can't wrap our minds around it without your help. Which brings us to…

Male Misconception: We Think You Have Rules

See, I just misconceived it right there in the last paragraph. Men think that you have rules. You don't. You have emotions. And emotions are fluid. You might say that you like something. We mentally jot that down, thinking we know something solid.

See, with our guy friends, we know where we stand: "Darryl doesn't like Chinese food. I won't bother to bring that up anymore." And then, if one day, Darryl says, "Let's go out for Chinese food," the man goes, "Oh, okay. Sometimes he likes Chinese food, sometimes he doesn't. And he'll tell me which time is which."

That's the difference. That's what we don't get. When you say that you don't want Chinese food, we don't know if you are saying

1. I don't like Chinese food.

2. I do like it, but I am not in the mood for it.

3. I love it, and I want it right now—but I am feeling fat, and I need you to play along and convince me that not only am I beautiful but that I can have

Chinese food and it will not make me fatter, and you will love me either way.

4. I really wish we were getting Italian food, but rather than saying that, I'll just say I don't want Chinese food and hope he figures out that means I want Italian... somehow.

And not only does it mean any of these or a hundred other things, but also you *know* which one it is. And we know that you know that. And we know that we don't know. And we fear that you know that we don't know.

Many men think that if we can understand enough of these situations, someday we will finally have you figured out. This is why men like working with technology. There is a rhyme and reason to it. If you push this button, this is what happens. Always. Women don't work that way, but we, for some reason, want to believe that they do—and so we'll never get it. Doesn't make sense, but we're still trying. I know for a fact that women don't work that way. I've been told many, many times (and sometimes I actually was listening). And yet even I am still trying to figure it out.

All I'm suggesting is to allow us to stop trying to figure you out. We probably should be able to. But we can't do it. We just can't. And we never will, so let us off the hook. Please accept us anyway. We tried to understand you without you telling us. We did it about a zillion times. We really did. And we hit about 50 percent of the time. About as often as if we flipped a coin.

If you can be as clear with us as possible, well, we'll still probably screw things up quite a bit. But at least it won't be about that. We'll find new things to screw up. And isn't that what life is all about? Finding newer and better things to fail at? Wait, it's not? Okay, then I've been doing this whole thing wrong.

Know That He Is Being Clear

This one isn't always easy for women to believe. But yes, men are rarely very sneaky about their feelings, desires, needs with you. If he calls you in the middle of the night to have sex and then you don't hear from him for three weeks, when he calls you again in the middle of the night to have sex, do not look for the deep meaning here. The meaning is that he only thinks of you every three weeks, when he is in the mood to have sex with you. It doesn't matter how great the sex is/was. It doesn't matter how sweet he talks on that phone call. His behavior tells you all you need to know.

The point is, *don't delve.* Just stop it. Don't try to imagine all the possible circumstances that are making him act however he is acting. If you are doing this, you are thinking too hard about it. Don't bother. Save your strength. Ask yourself, "Okay, if a creature that had *no* brain at all was behaving this way, why might it be doing it?"

Don't Try to Change Him

Every woman should have heard this one about a zillion times by now (at least a couple of times in this very book, if you were paying close attention), but it bears repeating. Number one, it never, *ever* works. And number two, it's not nice. That's what he's like. If you can't live with it, you're with the "wrong guy," not a "great new hobby."

And maybe, most importantly, you don't want this anyway. You don't want a guy who needs to change to become the person you want. That's not even fun. You want someone who fits well with you, even though you and he are so different. Which brings me to…

We Like All the Mystery

I know that secretly you *love* not knowing what he's thinking. And he loves not being able to figure you out. It's fun. And when you're with the right person, it's constantly surprising, sometimes frustrating, but all worth the trip.

Well, I suppose that is that, my delicate butterflies. I hope that at least one idea in this book has been helpful to you. Actually, I hope a lot more of them were, but I guess at least that number should not be zero.

I hope that you have a great time trying to figure this stuff out. Have fun—it's very satisfying to take the behavior of someone of the opposite sex and to translate it into something that you can understand and work with. The first time you do it, you will be so pleased with yourself, you won't be able to stand it. You will become drunk with power.

Regardless, I hope you find all the love and sex you can stand. And if by some bizarre, insane, barely worth mentioning, outside chance I haven't solved every single relationship problem you've ever had—ludicrous, I know!—hey, drop by my website, and I'll see what I can do.

THE END…
…OR IS IT ONLY THE BEGINNING…?
WELL… NO, IT'S PRETTY MUCH THE END.

As you can see below, we've got two sections, just like in a foreign language phrase book: Man-to-Woman and Woman-to-Man.*

MAN-TO-WOMAN (STUFF THAT HE SAYS)

He Says	Manslation
"That was fun, we'll have to do it again sometime."	Absolutely nothing. He could as easily have just done the Charlie Brown "wah *wah* wah *wah wah*" talk. He only said this to end the date without incident.
"I'm not a good boyfriend."	I've done something very, very wrong already or am planning on doing so. At the very least, I know that I don't trust myself, so you definitely should take my word for it. Bail out now.

---

* I imagine that's what those phrase books are like. I took Latin, for which they don't bother making phrase books, since your chances of meeting either (a) the pope or (b) an ancient Roman centurion are pretty slim.

He Says	Manslation
"I don't care where we go for dinner."	Oh please, God, will you please make up your mind? I'm dying over here. I really *do not* care where we go, and so I want you to make the decision in case you do. If you don't, let's just go *any* freaking where.
"What? Honey, of course I don't find HER attractive."	I do find her attractive, and the sexual part of my brain was just thinking about her naked. Please stop asking about this, you don't wanna know.
"I give great backrubs."	Please, if you have sex with me, I'll do everything I can to make you like it.*
"You should come check out my (insert name of attraction—riverview apartment, sailboat, marmot ranch) sometime."	I would like you to have sex with me at my (insert name of attraction), and I'm hoping that if you go look at it with me, we can make that happen.
"I'm just not looking for a relationship right now."	I'm not looking for a relationship with *you* right now. (Even Hannibal Lecter's looking for a relationship right now. Granted, the one he's after will probably involve herbs and/or spices and preheating his oven, but the point stands.)

---
* This one is actually used by both genders.

He Says	Manslation
"I just got out of a relationship, and I don't think I'm ready."	I'm only recently single, and I'm not lonely enough right now to date you.
"I'm not looking for a real 'commitment' right now."	I'm looking for some sex, no strings attached, and I'm hoping you'll oblige me. However, I'm pretty sure you wouldn't go for it if I put it in those terms.
"I think of you as more of a friend."	I don't want to have sex with you.
"I want to… but I don't want to mess up our friendship."	I want to have sex, but I don't want to have any responsibility to you afterward.
"Look, I'm a passionate person…."	Expect all kinds of erratic behavior with no apologies.
"Well, I have ADD/Asperger's/ depression/etc., so…."	See "Look, I'm a passionate person…"
"That woman's shirt was really weird, did you see that?"	I was absolutely staring at that woman's boobs, and I'm just making sure I'm covered with an alibi if you spotted me doing it.
"Your friend—what was her name? She was really fun!"	I am picturing her naked right now.

He Says	Manslation
"I've been meaning to call you, but work just got crazy busy. We should hang out sometime."	Say it with me: *booty call!*
"I could never date a woman who is constantly asking, 'Am I fat? Do I look fat in this?'"	I have never been in a relationship longer than a month.
"We're basically broken up. In a way, we broke up a long time ago."	We broke up yesterday. Well, sort of. We're probably going to break up soon. Want to have sex?

WOMAN-TO-MAN (WHAT HE THINKS WHEN YOU SAY IT)

She Says	Manslation
"We have to talk"	Uh-oh, I'm in big trouble. What did I do? Quick, damage control! Get ready to say whatever gets us off the hook!
"Where do you see this relationship going?"	She wants to get married—*now*. Either that or she wants to break up—*now*.
"What are you thinking/feeling right now?"	(Insert that sound your TV makes after a station goes off the air.)
"Do you think she's attractive?"	Danger. Trick question. Quickly say, "No, God no, honey!" Do not, under any circumstances, pause to think!
"Do I look fat in this?"	Red alert! *Do not* look at her body. Just tell her *no no no*.
"Do you remember what I was wearing on our first date?"	Oh man, I'm screwed. I don't even remember what I'm wearing right now unless I look down and check.
"Notice anything different about me?" (i.e. fishing for a compliment on your new hairstyle/tattoo/piercing)	Okaaaaay… Let's see… what did she look like yesterday? Think, damn you, think!

She Says	Manslation
"Do you think you'll want to have kids someday?"	Her biological clock is about to punch me in the face.
"Can you please (insert name of chore you want him to do)?"	Okay, here's what we'll do: Say, "Sure, no problem." And that's it. Hopefully, this will all blow over and she'll forget we had this talk.
"Listen, can you please just actually do (insert name of same chore)?"	Okay, it's not going away. How can I do this without actually, you know, *doing* it?
"Will you please just ask someone for directions?"	Stay on target. We are not—repeat *not*—lost. We'll get there on our *own*. For we are mighty!

• acknowledgments

First of all, I'd be remiss if I didn't begin with major thanks to my editor, Shana Drehs and her intrepid assistant, Sara Kase over at Sourcebooks. Without these two geniuses steering the process, this book would have ended up the literary equivalent of me walking around all day with my fly unzipped. And not in a good way.

I want to thank my literary agent, the very badass Holly Bemiss, whose belief in this project and in me as a writer helped make this thing happen. And thanks so much to Erin for introducing me to Holly.

Special thanks to the unbelievably talented stand-up comic, Becky Donohue, who was one of the first manslatees and an early champion of my career as a comic.

A quick nod to JoAnn Grigioni at Comedy Central, who is singlehandedly destroying the image of the "industry douchebag" by somehow managing to be both fantastic at her job and also incredibly fun, nice, and human at the same time.

I'd also like to acknowledge Peter Hedges, a great writer and a great guy, who generously agreed to sit down and talk with me about how to go from "wanting to write" to "actually writing." (Not that I actually followed his completely sensible advice or anything... but hey, nobody ever said I had common sense. No, I mean literally nobody ever said that.)

I am especially grateful to Liz, without whom I probably wouldn't do much of anything at all.

• about the author

Jeff Mac was born and raised in Connecticut, but left as soon as he found out you were allowed to. He went to the North Carolina School of the Arts where a fantastic education in classical acting was almost completely wasted upon him. A true jack of no trades, Jeff has been a computer programmer, the voice of a roll of toilet paper in TV commercials, and a mock patient for the purposes of training medical students. He spent several years as a stand-up comic, and was ultimately featured on Comedy Central's *Live at Gotham*. He is, to date, the only winner of the Mr. Lower East Side Pageant ever to face an impeachment trial. Several less-than-perfect relationships (and one great one) later, Jeff writes dating advice for women at www.manslations.com. He lives in an absurdly small apartment in Brooklyn with his lovely lady.